IN PERPETUUM

The poetic journal of a Welsh Monk

Musings in a medieval cloister

1995–2000

by

DAVID JONES

ORIGINAL WRITING

ISBN: 978-1-906018-54-2

A CIP catalogue for this book is available from the National Library.

Published by Original Writing Ltd., Dublin, 2008.

Printed in Ireland by Cahill Printers Limited.

To read is to be with a buried word
That could have lain unheard – to be alone
And not alone where memories are stirred
On this the page that stores them as its own:
'Tis to be all at listen, all an ear
Of inward hearing well, to answer not
But to be taught beneath a bygone year
By one whose mast'ry did not with him rot.
To write is to speak well without a voice
Across the years that threaten, 'tis to be
A little careful in a little choice
Of shapes that hold a sound that some may see
Tomorrow and tomorrow where we are
Not seen again, but heard afar, afar.

FOREWORD

"To know that I am Thine, and Thine shall be"

PROBABLY IN OUR COMPUTER AGE, with all the facilities of web-sites in internet and the unending round of poetry competitions, there are more poets, poetasters and would-be poets than ever before. There may, however, well be less that have gone to the pains of learning their craft than in former times. Dom David Jones, the Welsh Monk, is not of this number. He has been writing steadily since the late 'seventies, and has emerged as a serious religious poet of considerable merit, who does not indulge in such sensational gambits as "having sex with God," which some contemporaries delude themselves is not only poetry but even "devout."

Born in Cardiff on 16 November 1953 to Welsh parents with considerable cultural interests, he was brought up in an ambience where religious practice played a considerable role in daily life. In 1967, in the lead-up to a Billy Graham summer campaign, he experienced an inner "conversion" and was baptised in the Baptist Chapel at Cardiff on 8 October 1967, assuming full membership of that community on 15 October. His indefatigable quest to know God was, however, only beginning. Soon his reading convinced him that the truth in all its fulness lay with the Roman Catholic Church, but, owing to his youth, his parents and mentors advised him to wait awhile before seeking admission, though he already tended to attend mass rather than the services in the local Baptist chapel. On Holy Saturday, 10 April 1971, he was, however, "reconciled" to the Catholic Church by Dom Edmund Hatton (novice master), on behalf of his spiritual director, Dom Laurence Bénevot, in St. David's chapel in the crypt of Ampleforth Abbey.

After taking his A levels in the summer of 1972, he stayed on at school till Easter 1973, so that he might learn Greek. With impulsive generosity he immediately wished to enter Prinknash Abbey near Gloucester, a community of Benedictines of the Primitive Observance, who enjoyed a reputation for austerity. However, in view of his recent conversion and the fact that he had been awarded a scholarship for university studies, he was advised to take his degree first and went off to study Latin, Greek and Philosophy at the University College of Wales in Aberystwyth, where he graduated with joint honours in Latin and Greek in 1976. His monastic journey then began in earnest. After a stay at La Grande Trappe in Normandy, he made a retreat at the charterhouse of Sélignac near Bourg-en-Bresse before entering the Carthusian Order on 20 December 1976. It was at Sélignac that Dom David, as he was called in religion, began after a time to write poetry seriously, taking for his material his inner experiences in his search for the divine. If some echoes of Wordsworth, Coleridge and Hopkins are apparent, the monk at once found his own voice, and the reader is left in no doubt as regards the immediacy of the experiences depicted in The Threshold of Paradise.[1] Eva Schmid-Mörwald, writing in the preface to Paradise Regained[2], reveals her reaction to this first volume:

When I first came across The Threshold of Paradise, a collection of verse written by a contemporary Welsh novice monk, I was

---

1 Anon., *The Threshold of Paradise: The Poetic Journal of a Welsh Novice Monk* , in *Analecta Cartusiana* 129 (1988), v-xii, 1-90. The volume was republished with a preface by the present writer and a blurb by Eva Schmid Mörwald as: A Monk, *The Threshold of Paradise*, Adelphi Press, London 1994. Some of the poems were also reprinted in A Welsh Novice Monk, *Poem Sacred and Profane, Salzburg Studies in English Literature, Poetic Drama & Poetic Theory* 68:3 (1988), 5-45.

2 Anon. [A Welsh Novice Monk], *Paradise Regained, Salzburg Studies in English Literature, Poetic Drama & Poetic Theory* 146 (1996), iii.

stirred by the enthralling spirit radiating from the poems. The novice's love and reverence for the Creator were startling. Here a man was celebrating his love for God by creating poems of subtle beauty. His happiness was not unblemished though, for the road to perfection is a long and stony path, as was reflected in the verse. These poems grippingly captured the circumstances of their origin and whilst reading them I was bound to grasp some of the enormous inner tension that must have been present at their origin. I could feel the poet's urge to express his feelings and find an outlet for them. My interest was aroused: poet AND monk? The lines I had been reading were no feeble attemps in versifying, for they had a voice of their own; however, the two concepts of being both a monk true to heaven and a poet true to earth seemed to be too different to blend, particularly as it was the work of a Carthusian monk I had been reading. Wasn't that a contradiction in itself? Could these two vocations really be successfully united, sustaining each other in perfect symbiosis without doing harm to one [an]other?

Brother David's monastic vocation is highly interwoven with his poetic vocation; there is a strong original link between his call to solitude and his urge to write poetry. For him the writing of poetry represents a means to praise his Creator but also serves as an outlet for accumulated feelings. The poet's urge to write is nurtured by his boundless belief in and love for God, the poems stem from the intensity of his religious experience. His first poetic volumes adopt the form of a diary, where we find poems as diary entries. They reflect the spiritual journey of their author in all its intensity and invite the reader to partake. Periods of unbound happiness and joy, when feeling the closeness to God, as well as times of appalling grief, disappointment and loneliness, when experiencing His absence, are captured in his verse, their honest straightforwardness leaving the reader dazed at times.[3]

3   In her blurb for Anon., *Ad Maiestatem: The Journal of a Welsh Monk*, *Salzburg Studies in English Literature, Poetic Drama & Poetic Theory* 146:2 (1997), she expresses similar sentiments: "His verse reflects the austere life in a Carthusian cell, mirroring a whole world which usually is firmly closed

The Threshold of Paradise indeed mirrors the devotion of a Carthusian monk and his inner struggles, offering glimpses of an austerity unequalled by any other Catholic Order. Unfortunately, the authorities of the Order felt—rightly or wrongly—that Dom David did not possess a purely Carthusian vocation, and, after his seven years of probation, he was not admitted to solemn vows, leaving the Order on 25 March 1984 on the expiration of his temporary vows.[4]

After a period of reflection, including retreats at Quarr Abbey and St. Hugh's Charterhouse near Horsham, Dom David decided to enter La Grande Trappe, a monastery that had always fascinated him. His volume A World within the World: The Poetic Journal of a Welsh Novice Monk[5] reflects his experiences as a Cistercian monk of the Strict Observance, but here again his aspirations were disappointed, despite the undoubted seriousness of his intentions, which are clearly revealed in such poems as "The twenty-fifth of March 1984."[6] The sonnet became his preferred verse-form for depicting his spiritual journey on the stony road to perfection. The chapter of La Grande Trappe held the opinion that writing

off from the rest of mankind outside the monastic walls. The firmness of his belief, assailed nevertheless by spiritual struggles, utmost despair as opposed to ecstatic happiness, the fruits of silence contrasted by desperate loneliness, represent an immensely fruitful source for his poetry ... his musings merge into a poetry not only of high spiritual value but also offer great æsthetic pleasure. The sonnet proves to be the poet's favourire verse form, a remarkable fact, as traditional verse forms, in particular such demanding ones as the sonnet, do not enjoy great popularity nowadays." Eva Schmid-Mörwald is also responsible for two major studies of Dom David's poetry: "Poetry in the Order: A Welsh Novice Monk", in James Hogg, Karl Hubmayer, & Dorothea Steiner (eds.), English Language and Literature: Positions and Dispositions, Salzburger Studien zur Anglistik und Amerikanistik 16 (1990), 73-82, and The Lyre and the Cross in the Poetry of Alun Idris Jones, Analecta Cartusiana 129:2 (1994), a study containing detailed analyses of the poems and furnishing an excellent bibliography.

4   Dom Augustin Devaux, La Poésie Latine chez les Chartreux, Analecta Cartusiana 131 (1997), reveals, however, that a fair number of Carthusians did indulge in writing poetry. He devotes pp. 426-29 to Dom David Jones.
5   Salzburg Studies in English Literature, Poetic Drama & Poetic Theory 68:2 (1988).
6   Printed in The Threshold of Paradise, Analecta Cartusiana edition, 90.

poetry was irreconcilable with the Cistercian vocation, so, after nearly two years of trial, he moved on to the Trappist abbey of Roscrea in Southern Ireland, hoping to find the monks there more sympathetic to his poetic bent. Unfortunately for him Roscrea is unusual in running a school, which inevitably diminishes the seclusion of the monks to a certain extent. He struggled on for a time, but eventually left and returned to Wales on 20 June 1986. Far from being disillusioned, he was full of plans, contemplating becoming a recluse or even trying to re-establish monastic life in North Wales. At other moments he thought of engaging in the Charismatic Renewal in France. As no concrete possibility offered itself, he resumed studies at the Normal College in Bangor on 8 September 1986, obtaining a graduate diploma in primary education the following year. The pull of the monastic life had by no means diminished, and he made retreats at a number of houses, before settling in for a prolonged stay at Ealing Abbey, a Benedictine house affiliated to the English Congregation in the suburbs of London. There he was advised to seek out a community more exclusively devoted to the contemplative life. Rather rashly, he chose Farnborough Abbey, not far from London, a house that had changed over from the Solesmes Congregation to that of Subiaco, but which somehow had never flourished. No doubt, he was attracted by the musical tradition of the monks. He began his official postulancy there on 7 March 1988 and was clothed in the Benedictine habit on 10 December of that year, the Feast of St. John Roberts, taking the name of that Saint. The young novice did not find Farnborough as congenial as he had hoped. The community was small and passed through a dolorous crisis. Furthermore, the monks were heavily engaged in looking after the parish, which reduced the time available for a more strictly contemplative life. Early in 1989 he realized that he would not find fulfilment there and returned to Wales, where he resided at Talacre Abbey with Dom Basil Heath-Robinson, the former prior of Farnborough, for five weeks, pondering on the possibility of initiating a Benedictine foundation in North Wales. Though the Abbot of Ramsgate, Dom Gilbert Jones, was favourable to the venture, the local bishop was unsympathetic and withheld his approval. From April onwards the poet was enlisted on a project for translating the Church Fathers into Modern English.[7] At the start of the new academic year, in the autumn of 1989, the poet enlisted for the Bachelor of Divinity course at University College, Bangor. Owing to his previous studies he was allowed to condense the three years into two, graduating in June 1991. Meanwhile he had been reflecting on the future. His spiritual director, Dr. John Ryan, O.M.I., felt that the Premonstratensian Order, with its ordered liturgy and tradition of study and prayer in community, might be the long sought-for haven. He established contacts with Holy Trinity Abbey at Kilnacrott in County Cavan, Ireland. The poet entered this community on the Feast of St. Luke, 18 October 1991, and took the habit on the Feast of the Immaculate Conception, celebrated on 9 December that year. He reverted to the religious name Dom David. After the first year of his novitiate he recommenced theological studies in Dublin. The volume A World beyond the World[8] depicts his experiences at Farnborough, his time as a student at Bangor, and his novitiate at Kilnacrott. Inevitably, student life reveals different atmospherics to the daily round of the cloister, but his unalloyed joy at re-entering the religious life, where he might devote himself to God alone, is unmistakable. On 8 December 1993 he made his profession as a Premonstratensian. A few weeks later, on 30 January 1994, he was sent to study Spritual Theology at the Angelicum in Rome, residing at the Premonstratensian house in the eternal city. He had learnt enough Italian in Dublin to get by, and as the canons at Kilnacrott engaged in pastoral and youth work, it was felt that such a course of study would be helpful to him in counselling work later. At last, all seemed to have settled to a calm, which is reflected in his poems of the time, but further tempests were brewing up. Kilnacrott hit the headlines in the national press as a result of an unfortunate scandal. The superior was changed and

---

7   This resulted in Oliver Davies, *Promise of Good Things. The Apostolic Fathers*. Translations by Alun Idris Jones and Oliver Davies, London 1992.
8   *Analecta Cartusiana* 129:3 (1993).

even the future of the abbey seemed in jeopardy. He was able to present his minor thesis in the early summer of 1995,[9] but was then ordered to return to Ireland. He obeyed, leaving Rome on 18 June, but, owing to the turmoil at the abbey, he requested six months' leave of absence to reflect upon the situation. This was granted and Dom David resided for a time at Mount Tabor Hermitage in the west of Ireland, which had recently been consecrated by the Archbishop of Tuam. The solution could only be temporary, as he was not yet in Holy Orders, and therefore could not really act as chaplain. That summer my wife and I had by chance visited the magnificent romanesque abbey of Sant'Antimo, in a remote corner of Tuscany, where a small community, mainly from France, follow the Premonstratensian rule and sing the whole of the Office to the original Gregorian melodies in Latin in the abbey church. We were duly impressed, and, knowing of the crisis at Kilnacrott, we suggested to Dom David that this might be something for him. He duly arrived at the Abbazia near Castelnuovo dell'Abate on 6 December 1995, and though he hesitated to leave the official Premonstratensian Order for some weeks, as several poems in the present volume reveal,[10] he finally decided to join the community at Sant'Antimo, where he made his solemn profession on 9 December 1996, and was ordained to the priesthood in Siena's beautiful medieval cathedral on 31 October 1997. Soon thereafter he returned to the Angelicum, where he presented a doctoral thesis of the highest distinction in December 1998.[11] He now occupies the combined posts of sacristan and guest-master at Sant'Antimo, and since March 2000 has also been given charge of the noviciate.

---

9   This has been printed as Br. David Jones, "Adam Scot: The tension in the psyche of the man of prayer between active and contemplative life", in *The Mystical Tradition and the Carthusians, Analecta Cartusiana* 130:11 (1996), 1-37.

10   Cf. particularly the poem "Rome".

11   Printed as Br. David Jones, *An Early Witness to the Nature of the Canonical Order in the Twelfth Century: A Study in the Life and Writings of Adam Scot, with Particular Reference to his Understanding of the Rule of St. Augustine, Analecta Cartusiana* 151 (1999).

Some poems from this period were printed in Ad Maiestatem,[1] but this new collection gives a much more detailed overall picture of the poet's spiritual pilgrimage from the time of his first studies in Rome up to the present. A much greater tranquillity is immediately apparent, even if some longings remain unsatisfied.

As in previous volumes, the poet shows himself to be an expert linguist, writing with equal facility in Welsh, English, French, Italian, Latin and Greek. There are no poems as yet in German, though there are several German headings, and after residences at Wilten Abbey near Innsbruck and with the Benedictines in Augsburg to learn the language, it only seems a matter of time before he tries his hand in that language too.

Dom David is not an avant-garde poet. In some respects the poems in the slim volume recently issued for a monk of Parkminster are more "modern" in their texture, but the slightly archaic tone on occasion has been deliberately chosen as appropriate to clothe the religious content. The topics are almost exclusively concerned with the daily round of the religious life, and we see the poet learning to say the mass, listen to his innermost thoughts about his profession and ordination, his joy in celebrating the mass in abbeys and churches that had meant much to him in the past, his administering the sacraments and preaching retreats, even as far away as at a nunnery in Rumania, his enthusiasm for pilgrimages such as Medugorje, which the present writer has always felt rather reserved about, as also for Dom David's enthusiasm for miracles, wonders and signs.[13] Even after his ordination, he was still dreaming of restoring the monastic life in Wales, as "Penmon" reveals, and his fascination with the solitary life as led by the Carthusian and Camaldolese Orders remained, as we see in "This is the day," "A New Reverend Father," "Chartreuse," "Letter from the Grande Chartreuse," "Unopened," "Eve of Saint Romuald," "Recluso,"

---

12 Several poems are reprinted in the present volume.
13 This enthusiasm was apparent in earlier volumes of verse and in Alun Idris Jones, *The Purgatory Manuscript. Le Manuscrit du Purgatoire, Studies in Women and Religion* 29, Lewiston, N.Y. 1990.

"Eremo," "Dom Damien,"[14] "Reading lines penned beside Dom Damien's tomb," "Haunted," and "Letter to a friend."

It may be significant that, despite its French title,[15] he chose to write his profession poem in Welsh. However, there are poems in English revealing the depths of his feelings about his profession and ordination, which cannot fail to move the reader:

Vous avez été accepté
(à l'unanimité)

O! joy on earth! O! joy yet in the world!
To know that I am Thine, and Thine shall be,
And Thine alone, and by a little word
Upon this altar placed, eternally
To this Thy temple joined—to know that now
No man or angel fiend can mar the road
Trod here by friends now crowned, that once did bow
Here where I place my head: to see the cloud
Of witnesses unseen walk calmly by
And chuckle at an æon, to see all
Melt in a moment felt, nay, and to cry
A tear of blissful peace—this is to call
From out of the abyss of Failure vast,
And clutch at but a notch of grace at last.

or:

In petram inaccessam mihi deduc me

O joy! I shall yet hold Thee in my hand
Upon this ancient stone where others felt
The passing of their God: I shall there stand

---

14   Dom Damien had been a Carthusian at Sélignac, but he transferred to Camaldoli and died as a recluse there.

15   "Vous ferez la profession le neuf décembre", reflecting the Prior's own words.

Where souls have stood before and angels knelt
At veilèd Mystery—I see the light
Of Tabor in this night, for this one word
Of manhood made is weighed with Godhead's might,
And in one chrismic sound I have all heard.
O Master of this astral path we tread,
I hear, I hear the voice that never was
By mortals caught, and here my little head
I bow to Thy great blessing: this day has
A ray of touch electric hither sent,
And o'er a sound the heavy cosmos bent.

or:

How beautiful are the feet of those who bear good tidings

[Prior's news of Dom David's ordination]
"C'est un des jours les plus heureux de ma vie!"

O! bliss in but a sound! O! happy day,
That changes every day for evermore,
That brings back yesterday from far away,
And sparkles with a grace once known before!
A word this hour was heard that has a pow'r
Beyond the noise of scribblings and of hands
Not driven from above; nay, one small hour
O'er years of heavy waiting calmly stands.
My God, I shall Thee touch, I shall Thee hold,
And be Thy voice on earth—I shall be free
To climb these ancient steps and there be bold
To walk alone 'mid clouded Trinity.
I shall, hid Friend, for ever and a day,
A Priest be, till the æons fade away.

Less exclusively autobiographical, and therefore applicable to
us all in these days of super-activism, is:

What is this life?

("J'ai gaspillé ma vie à faire trop de choses . . .")
(Paroles d'un Chartreux)

There is too much to do on earth, and more
Than need be done is done by all that do
Too much to do all well, for this one law
Of patient moments old, that ancients knew,
The new-found sound of man can ill contain,
And waning is the moon that should have known
To slowly be, to wholly be again
What once it calmly was to days outblown.
O Master of the energies of flesh,
That twitch and chatter o'er a loudest day
That held a bulging load, what did enmesh
The very brain that breathed, till it should pay
A debt too heavy to a great machine
That had no pow'r to stop till all had been?

The present volume not only offers a graphic portrayal of the
pilgrimage of a soul willingly and unreservedly placed in God's
hands in often arrestingly beautiful poetic diction, but also exudes
much sane wisdom, from which the modern reader, whatever his
religious commitment or lack of it, can profit.

Ash Wednesday 2000
James Hogg
University of Salzburg

'Απορία

O Silence in the sky, and upon earth
Unheard responses long! What holds the land
Of pilgrim sojourn here for one whose mirth
Lies where no eyes can peer, and where no hand
Can touch but One alone whose touching soft
Hath pulled and pulled thus far? O Guide all hid,
Where wilt thou have me walk, for turning oft
Upon this track, I have not heard Thee bid.
O Darkness of all time, where is the star
That glistened in the dawn, for morn is gone,
And evening by oft falling soon shall mar
The beauty of a dream too oft undone.
O Heaven, move this earth, for I can do
No more where man, it seems, can God undo.

9/11/95

I

Two letters from Erin

*(one from friends with land,
the other from a cardinal)*

When in the dark there is no mark or sound
To show the way to take; when there is none
That utters aught, and neither ear is found
Nor eye to gaze at all within undone;
When silence is too long where longing lurks
To be somewhere somehow already made
What we were meant to be, and when naught works
In this great engine wherein fate is played:
Then in a little paper there is weight
And sound of calling high; there is in print
Tapped by a red-capped wizard Magic's trait
That of æonic Vision bears some hint.
For though, my Lord, this stillness is too still,
A little hand can hold a Godhead's will.

Prémontré

*(A letter from Rome
and another from Sant'Antimo)*

Saint Norbert, to be 'neath thy mantle yet
And bathed in ancient light – to linger on
A little longer where the ages met
Upon a dot or two not wholly done
But chanted evermore – Ah! Melody!
To hear thee come again across the years
And call me home where wingèd custody
Can hold me bound and safe from freedom's fears:
'Tis to be tugged by one last cord too strong
To be so quickly snipped, for dipped am I
Not in a nocturn rave, but matins long
That have oft sunk 'neath soft Oblivion's sky.
I cannot leave, I cannot leave this land
Of foreshown beauty that becks one last hand.

Letter-opener

(Irish yew, 2,000 years old)

The years sapped by this trunk have passed us by
And yet remain to ope the sealèd space
Of slender thinking packed, that th'anguished eye
Will hear vibrate as e'en the distant face
Unseen peers loudly through the silent page,
And strokes or stabs the innards that feel all –
The years, I say, are here, for though we age,
We have the pow'r from hour to hour to call.
And in this gentle slitting of one day
Let yesterday to lie, there is a throng
Of myst'ries hid, for what one page will say
Will in our hist'ry's furrow linger long.
And what we are and will have been will be
Revealed, small tool, nay, for aye sealed by thee.

Genealogy

'Neath every headstone lies a history
And future that ends not where each thin line
Stops on this plotted shart, for mystery
Speaks for a silence vast where passed this fine
And slender thread of Being handed on
By many lying still – nay, one small grave
Holds fast eternity where time has gone
Beneath the billows choked by one last wave.
A scratch or two upon this page we are,
And we must journey on, yet sadness knows
A little gladness in our going far,
For in a trammelled glory something glows.
And I perceive that nothing upon earth
Can matter save one Matter of some worth.

Interpellé

(par les aïeux)

And some there were among these etchèd lines
That stood in pulpits large and beckoned well
To others on the road that fate entwines
With ways and by-ways weaved by peevèd Hell –
That stood, I say, where eyes were calmly poised
'Twixt work and work and days and passing days,
And for a little hour a rumour noised
That there were yet in darkness many rays.
These came and went, but did not pass alone
Into that spectred land, but holding still
A myriad in their clutch, 'neath this long stone,
They could their eyelids fasten to none ill.
For in this vale they shepherded much time,
And these old steps I sense their child must climb.

Bouleversé

(par la lettre de S. Antimo)

When at the hour of noon we stand and gaze
At our morn passing by, when we behold
Before our feet the parting of two ways
And from the eve its pattern yet withhold,
And when within we hear a kindred soul
Sigh, "Come this way and rest with us awhile,
For in the written part I see the whole,"
And when 'tis in one "Yea" to end this trial,
Then there is one "Amen" that would but come
Tomorrow for all time, were't not for this
Small particle of earth that is yet home,
For that it holds the faces of old bliss.
And though, my Lord, I catch this incense spell,
Which cloud was sent by Thee I cannot tell.

Y Saboth olaf

*(Last Sabbath in Wales,
after latest kind message)*

From home to home we wander in this world,
Yet home is not herein, for Paradise
Was not of mortar made, and to be hurled
Into an orbit wide is 'neath the skies
To have no heav'n our own: we were not made
To linger long in loving upon earth,
And where the fondest features slowly fade
We sense not rest where sense alone is mirth.
But I have seen a glimmer on this hill,
Of newness very old, and boldness here
Will crack an ancient wonder: here I will,
In incense dense, of Godhead have no fear,
But rest upon this altar my tired head,
And make my home there where Another bled.

Reclothed

O Saint of God, that from a Virgin's hand
Didst bear this cloth now giv'n again to one
That roved too long from land to distant land
Without a home beneath this ageing sun,
Wouldst thou here bid me halt and take the pain
Of exile as the heavy cross to be
The part of one alone, nay, and again
This cold well known as all mine ecstasy?
O rapture, wait awhile. I will walk on
A little longer on this well trod way,
For though all sound familiar is now gone,
There is a little glimmer in this day
That dawns upon an altar standing high
Upon an ancient dream now drawing nigh.

Ange en prière

Ô petit rien voilé par la nuit
De nos regards inachevés, pourquoi
Venir briser encor ce que je suis
Par ce que, seul, tu es, par ce que, toi,
Tu es sans bruit ni son ni gloriole
Qui, pourtant, t'appartient, car seule ici
Avec ton seul Ami, tu es parole
De vérité écoutée et saisie.
O! cœur qui parle et bat pour un seul Cœur!
Tu passeras sans doute en ce demain
Qui portera tes traces, mais, vraie sœur,
Revêtue par les anges, tends la main,
Car j'entre dans la nuit, moi seul, aussi
Et Demain ne te verra plus ici.

Completi sunt

Today is but another yesterday
Tomorrow yet to come, and this old year
Was new a while ago, and yet for aye
There is but one wide moment standing here
Upon the which we walk, and there is none
Shall travel other wise, for all the earth
Together plots its course upon this sun
That calls the minutes of our pain and mirth.
O Morrow hugely hid! What bids this night
From its dark entrails come? Where will this hour
Of midnight strike again when one year's light
Fades 'neath the heavy slumber of time's pow'r?
And will this incense sweet yet fill the air
Of this strange call that bids me settle ne'er?

Je reste

Ô doigt de Dieu, qui tourne l'univers
Et meus le cœur de l'homme, je te sens
En cette nuit enfin où par ces vers
Le grand Amen se dit, car maintenant
Je sais à Qui je viens, je connais bien
La route ancienne que cet avenir
Contient, car je suis tenu par un lien
Plus fort que ce qui pourrait me tenir.
O! joie d'Amour, de dernier abandon,
De folie qui crie "Tout!"—je veux Te voir
Enfin, grand Dieu, là où l'ultime don
Me place dans la paix d'un nouveau soir
Fait tout de lendemains où Tu seras
Le seul qui dorénavant comptera.

Rome

"Leave not the fold," they said, "ere thou hast
heard
The voice of one more shepherd who can see
With vision better placet; hear one more word
That can in coming save thy destiny
From found'ring well, for something hugely dark
Hangs o'er this whitened way, and in one day
Thou canst nine cent'ries let slip 'yond the mark
Of one life's last recall with this light play."
O! pain of double hurt! I cannot be
Upon two parts of earth, or hear this sound
Of echoed history and still be free
To tread again its path where once 'twas found.
O Norbert, look again! I see not well,
For 'tis a day that morrows all will tell.

Surrender

O! Beauty ever old and ever new
That travels on the air of yesteryear!
I cannot leave again this land I knew
When love was strong, and Song did lull the ear
With meanings of its own—I cannot be
Afar from where I am, for there is more
Within a little space that shelters me
From trudgings long than one strong hingèd door:
There is upon this stone a home where God
Can in my hand be born, there is a place
Hard by a softer light where Brightness trod
A path into my heart—for this Thy Face
I feel upon me beaming in the night,
And I'll not leave this land of loving quite.

Vixit

Y mae i bapur mud ryw adlais clir,
Ac i lythrennau mân rai creithiau sydd
Yn torri drwy'r hyn ŷm—y mae i'r gwir
Ryw allu dros yr awr a'r oriau fydd
Yn treiddio 'fory'r rhod, a nod y graith
Sydd ar y ddalen hon a erys dro
Ar wyneb haul a lloer boreau maith
Na welant wedd yr hun sydd dan y gro.
Yfory ni fydd inc a ddaw yn ôl
Ag odl o'r tir pell lle'r erys oll
Yn ddistaw a di-sill, a synau ffôl
Ein synied am a fydd i ti sy'ngholl,
Ein cyfaill cu, a fuost am fer awr
Yn llewyrch brau o wenau Blaen y Wawr.

(Rev Emrys Edwards, a neighbour and
friend, used to correspond with me in verse.)

Caterina

O fun yn un â Duw, yn fwy na dyn,
Yn ddynes yn dy gorff ond yn dy ddawn
Yn fugail i'r pen fugail mawr ei hun,
Ac yn dy gnawd yn newydd gnawd i'r Iawn—
A gofi heddiw'r cerrig henaidd hyn
Lle safodd gynt dy droed, a'r oed lle bu
I fintai gref at wyry wen yn syn
Ymsymud heb na sain na murmur su?
A glywi heno, chwaer, yn nef y nef
Yr hen gyfaredd hon sy'n dod yn ôl
O garreg ac o garreg lle bu llef
Sawl pell golledig sant yn nefol ffôl
Yn llenwi gofod gwag â seiniau mân,
Yn llenwi gofod oes â hen, hen gân?

Un être te manque,
et tout est dépeuplé

To think and think again on what has been,
And to recall an hour when all was lost;
To see again the eyes that are not seen,
And to behold one moment that all tossed;
To utter oft within the breast soft sounds
That by none here below will e'er be heard,
And to be bound by sorrow that no bounds
Can hold or soften by an answered word:
This is, my friend, hence silent to the end
Of these our parted days—this is to be
A sadness that no morrow now can mend,
For that the sight of one it shall not see:
The face of one that held awhile the world
Was on a day to darkened days e'er hurled.

Reçu

O! sorrow evermore and nevermore
To be alone here held—I am where love
Can in a fond embrace as once before
My calmèd soul enlace: I hear above
This altar where we'll meet a gentle breeze
All of a Presence made, I hear again
Upon the tranquil night what no eye sees,
For in one word is heard an end of pain.
O Master, I will come and Thee ere long
Hold o'er the world 'mid echoes of fair tune,
And in the morrows of this ancient song
I will hold well the rays of this last boon,
For love has called me here, and I shall stay
Until one fondness lost has passed away.

Enough

A cell is but a wall or two of stone
Of nothing made, with nothing weighed but air,
And there is neither face nor voice to own
The little man that can but ponder there,
And yet there can be in an emptiness
A sound that oft was found upon this shore
Of seconds that we tread, where blessedness
Laps for a while our land as once of yore.
For I can hear, my Lord, within this place
A rhythm that I know, and I can tell
The meaning in the look of this Thy Face
That I see not, for man sees not here well,
Yet there is here enough for one to be
A salvaged morsel of eternity.

"Dñs Hugo fecit nos fieri omnis Alpha et Omega

Anno Dñi MCCXVIII"

Ring out again upon these Tuscan hills
Your brazen song of measured tempo known
By oft a passing ear, with sound that stills
The moving of all time, for in this stone
That hears again the echo that your call
Draws hourly from our breasts, there lingers yet
A wonder of long finding: something small
In this your poisèd stroke holds hours long set.
O! souls that flew this way and glided on
To where this sun now sets—O! westward clan,
That lies in skelet form where days have gone
Beneath this tapping of the tune of Man—Await a little
onthis patient shore
Of minutes that have lapped this land before.

Cassé

O maid and mother, known to one alone,
Who once had heard thy song and known thy
voice
Upon a lonely land that two did own
A little while, what was this unthought choice
That chose all time asunder to be held
And to be made to be what it shall be
For ever, ever more—what thus withheld
What could have calmly been all history?
O little one now lost, now tossed away,
Why didst thou pause not at the morrow's door
That in a mighty moment on a day
In one strong strident second all things bore?
O! woman kind, so kind and cruel to man,
You wave a wand that no known Godhead can.

Yesterday

When I recall the voice that called my name
Across the Hibern wind, when I behold
Again upon the mem'ry's screen the dame
That o'er my hermit's dream all sway did hold,
And when I hear the cantress in the air
The praise of glory 'mid the incense bring
To Godhead's list'ning ears—when I tread there
Yet never there again shall ought e'er sing—Then in this
Tuscan cell, 'neath hooded thought
All of an echo made, I hear too much
For one shaved head to bear, for I hear nought
Of what the figment's image would fain clutch
A little while again, were it not so,
The pow'r of yesterday its way to go.

For ever

O! peace! O! peace! To know that we have found
A corner of the cosmos wherein all
May safely lie at rest, where naught but sound
Of gentle yestertone may henceforth fall
Upon the troubled ear, where we may be
Alone for love alone where all the world
May hear no more our voice or ever see
The heart that beats herein upon a word –
To know, O Logic hid, that Thou art there,
Amid the maddest course that brought us here,
And to feel tingle something in the air
Of incense dense where Godhead travels near:
This is to rest awhile upon a Breast
Whereon the æons yawned lie 'yond the West.

In petram inaccessam mihi deduc me

O joy! I shall yet hold Thee in my hand
Upon this ancient stone where others felt
The passing of their God: I shall there stand
Where souls have stood before and angels knelt
At veilèd Mystery – I see the light
Of Tabor in this night, for this one word
Of manhood made is weighed with Godhead's might,
And in one chrismic sound I have all heard.
O Master of this astral path we tread,
I hear, I hear the voice that never was
By mortals caught, and here my little head
I bow to Thy great blessing: this day has
A ray of touch electric hither sent,
And o'er a sound the heavy cosmos bent.

(After Fr Prior's return from Siena, with the news
from the Archbishop about Profession and Ordination.)

Spectaculum silentii

*(Gazing, after Compline, at
the brilliant comet)*

What is a soul upon the universe
That holds the all of all? What is a breath
Of being lent and sent too oft to curse
The hand of its fair Giver? What is death
Upon the cosmic path that all must tread
Where no feet walk again or backward stroll?
And in the land where none, 'tis often said,
Is heard again to speak, how will years roll?
And when we have burnt well our little star
And turn here, homeward bound, our blurring
gaze,
Will this track seem at length a little far
O'er ways galactic and undawnèd days?
And will there be an echo of this song
Upon that shore of memories too long?

Rhagluniaeth fawr y nef...

(After carrying the sacred Chrism in Siena)

Ni all y ddamwain hon fod dan ryw ffawd
Na welodd ac na threfnodd neb a fu
Yn syllu gynt ar hynt eonau'r rhawd
A welwyd ddoe ac echdoe oddi fry...
Gwn, Iôr, wrth deimlo'r deigryn hwn a ddaeth
Drwy waith cyfuniad hap a chyffwrdd ffôl
Ergydion Siawns, mai'r Iawn ei hun a aeth
Drwy'r dwylo hyn, cans yma dof yn ôl –
Yn ôl, fy Nhad, i'r Achos mawr ei hun,
Yn ôl i'r geiriau hen, i'r henaidd gof
Am goffadwraeth oes, am gof am Un
A etyb 'fory 'ngwŷs, cans heno dof
Â'r olew a'm heneinia'n un ag Ef,
A fynn fenthyca hyn o ddynol lef.

'Ανάξιος μοναχός Βαρναβάς

Bu dydd a dyddiau maith yn rhan o hwn,
Yr olaf air o hen epistol brau
Un einioes driw, fy Nhad yn Nuw – ond gwn
Nad damwain oedd y ddoe, ac aros mae
Yr anwes na fydd mwy, cans llais dy gân
Ac arogl dy thus a dreiddia dro
Yfory ac yfory dyllau mân
Y cof a edwyn gwmni pell y gro.
O! deulu'r Ddirgel Len, lle clywir mwy
Na'r hyn ddeil byddar glust, un Ust a fydd
Yn osteg i'ch holl sain: hyn dreiddia drwy
Yr olaf ddwfn "oes oesoedd" glôdd un dydd.
Ac ni fydd rhwng dwy linell seiniau hoff
Mwyn Dad ddug mab drwy gwmwl Iafe'n gloff.

No reply

O maid that marred the world, yet made it be
A miracle of moments running high
Upon the crest of sorrow, where the plea
For but one moment missed remained the sigh
Of broken hours e'ermore – O! child before
Well known and owned for aye ere this great sea
Of seconds huge lashed on this little shore
Of words ill heard, what dimmed this ecstasy:
The trancèd wonder of the rested bliss
That throbbed with scarce a sound, where two
had found
The cloud in which to live? What trampled this
Untrammelled astral path, where earth's last
bound,
We said, would halt us not, for to thy grave
I'd vowed each day to come, thy soul to crave?

Why?

O! pain! O! pain! O! fondness that ne'er was
As deep as it is now that 'tis no more –
O! plainness of known truth that nothing has
Been loud enough to muffle or pass o'er!
What shall yet be, when nothing may yet be
Of what alone meant most? What host of pains
Will hurt again tomorrow, when to see
The morrow that was not alone remains?
O! virgin filled with God that trod this way
And lay with Him within my breast one hour,
Was it for this that one long damnèd day
Did dawn from the abyss of Craft's foul pow'r?
Is this yet true, this truth I can't believe,
That one marred hour the æons all must cleave?

Eve of Saint Romuald

This is the day I came to thee, sweet soul;
This is the day, the hour, wherein a cloud
Bid two worlds briefly meet, when one maid's rôle
Did many others take, for I had vowed
My feet to this lost paradise to turn
Again, fond dream – to where in peace did tread
Thy piercèd feet that on that hill did learn
The skill of Celtic pain that virgins shred.
O martyr of fond loving that no heart
Again on earth may hear, fade now and die
Upon this stage of thinking whose one part,
Now parted for all time, left but a sigh
Too deep for tears, too deep for anything,
For there is hurt in much remembering.

Recluso

O Romuald, so near and now so far!
What would I give or sacrifice anon
One hour to spend again where now yet are
These poltergeists that haunt where once they won
The clouds they e'ermore tread! What would I do
To hack at this clock face to make it turn
A morrow into mist of mem'ries true
One only hour, th'hour hours, all hours, shall yearn!
O sound of softest sealing! I'd tread yet
This step to maddest dark, for saddest things
Are mended in the night, and I'd reset
This finger that drives all, for small sound brings
Unbounded pains, where ticks indelible
Have pow'r o'er all the world twice audible.

Amma, Amma

Another soul there will not be again
To whom my thought will go without a word,
Nor will a heart on earth e'er know the pain
That in a sound once heard will e'er be heard
In its unanswered calling. There is more
In sharing one small dream that came the way
Of two on this vast globe than what we bore
In many ravèd nights unheard of day.
For, sister of the night that heard our song
Ere dawned the sorrow that must linger on,
I thought our soft melisma would be long,
As long as was the breath of moine and nonne.
But dreams are shattered on this jagged shore
Of westward light that travelled on before.

Still no reply

What 'tis to wait and wait for but a word
That comes not hither on the wings of thought;
What 'tis to hear no more a voice once heard
Amid the one deep silence two had sought;
What 'tis, I say, each day a hungered look
To cast upon a little box not filled
With messages soft penned, where something
took
From this life's sky the face that all pain stilled:
Alone this weight of wanting much can tell,
For that not e'en the wanted shall e'er know,
And this long wait the dawn of Heav'n or Hell
Must bide ere something hide this last keen glow.
For I can not stop hurting here on earth,
When I'll see ne'er again the face of mirth.

Eremo
(After visit to St Romuald's hermitage)

To be again alone, to be again
What we can not but be – to be, to be
Alive at last with Being: to regain
The all once shed for aye where we did see
So little 'yond the day that all days marred –
To tread once more on this untrodden shore
Of hours and moments long, where glisters starred
Afar and very near as oft before:
Aha! 'Twould be the uttermost of Home
Soft shining in this night, 'twould be the day
Wherein again all days e'ermore to come
Would whisper, "'Twill not pass away..."
O! pain so huge! This yearning lingers long,
And though this chant be fair, one note is wrong.

This is the place
*(where happened the miracle that in ado-
lescence made me think)*

Dumb beast that taught the world without a word
The Word to heed, therewith to bend the knee:
'Twas this thine inward thinking that I heard,
This thy clear vision that I once did see
Through gazing on a page, wherein the age
Of Reason ceased to be, for all was said,
Good mule, that altered more than any sage
In this thy strangest greeting of strange Bread.
'Twas but a day like this that came this way
All days with but a neigh for aye to bend,
And now I see, blest preacher, that thy bray
A volume of hid sermons here did end,
And that a little particle would hold
Enough to groom a shepherd for the fold.

Vous ferez profession le neuf décembre

(veille de la fête de S. John Roberts)

Dychwelyd at y parthau tawel hyn,
Lle buost gynt, lle buom ninnau'n troi
Ein traed at lwybrau hedd, fwyn ferthyr gwyn,
Cyn i'n llencyndod a'n moryndod ffoi
At alltud ffawd, at rawd a'n llyncodd oll
I ebargofiant llwyr, lle na ŵyr neb
Am ddeigryn cudd na mân ochenaid coll
Am wyneb hoff, neu gof yr un sy' heb
Na chymar na chymarus enaid mwy
Ar noson hir, lle clywid unwaith sain
Rhyw lais adawodd graith ac anferth glwy'
Dyheu am hen gyfaredd llafar plaen –
Dychwelyd, wyryf gâr, hyn fyddai fwyn,
Ond y mae Un a all dy garu ddwyn.

Miracle
(qui scella ma conversion)

Ô trace de mon Dieu, ô lieu d'antan
Où Lui, l'Ancien des Jours, a mis ses pas
Une heure, un moment, un court maintenant
Que demain et demain reportera
Au dernier soir du monde... Ô trace immonde
Essuyé par nul ange, ô gaspillage
De grâce déguisée qui surabonde
Ainsi pour un seul cœur qu'on crut si sage:
Ce fut ton œil, ô voyant inconnu,
Qui voyait à ma place, et cette foi
Douteuse, qui en l'instant reconnut
L'Auteur et le Fauteur de toute loi
Pour toute heure à venir, saura percer
Ce voile qui dit tout sans insister.

The blood-stained corporal
(Bolsena - Orvieto)

O place wherein the Face of Godhead beamed
And shook the earth! O mirth of angels' smile,
That gazed, all, all amazed as droplets streamed
From matter badly formed, deformed awhile
By passing rays of Glory! Story vast!
In but a moment told, a moment old,
As old as this old tale told as the last
Of yesterday's long follies sweetly bold –
O madness of a God! Here trod those feet
That once in ancient time climbed 'twixt the skies
And that emblazoned chalice that this sheet
Veiled well from man, from mind, from grasping eyes,
And pattered once too loudly for one bread
To linger as ne'er stronger word were said.

Travail d'humilité
(avec une moniale cloîtrée)

Ô petit rien passé par ici
Sans savoir où tu allais, où ton Dieu
Voulais te voir, sais-tu qu'une heure ainsi
Partagée en ce coin obscur, ce lieu
De long exil, m'a mis un moment là
Où hier encor j'étais, où étaient deux
Unis en cette peine qu'ici-bas
Un monde porte sous ces mêmes cieux –
Sais-tu, belle âme, qu'en ta douce voix
Une autre est revenue, sais-tu que tout
Me parlait, me reparlait cette fois
Comme autrefois tout parlait entre nous
Anachorètes d'une extase brève
Qui me perça, me percera, sans trêve?

In search of water
(in the well our fathers dug)

We work upon an ancient work of old,
Old, oldest work of man; we dig for life
Upon the deep of death, the region cold
Of sleep and slumber long wherein the strife
Of every blow slow-heaved is now at rest
And shall be evermore – we probe the land
Of Passing wherein oft a hurried guest
Did meet the magic tapping of this wand...
O! tick of tugging pull, poised o'er a well
Of hollowed, hallowed echoes, clang anon
Upon the depths you pierce, and fiercest Hell
Confound by this one sound that lingers on:
For I perceive that you receive the all
That on this earth for gougèd mirth did crawl.

Petite sainte, enfin je te retrouve

Amie d'enfance, âme autrefois connue
Sur ce chemin parcouru par tant d'anges
Inaperçus, à jamais inconnus,
Mais mêlés désormais à ces phalanges
Qui seuls seront reconnus par ce monde
Qui dure – Ô! pure et claire voie
Aux astres qui demeurent, sur cette onde
D'encens longtemps laissé je t'entrevois:
Ô! chemin sûr d'antan, je sens les traces
De celles qui ont mis ici leur pas
Un jour où deux d'attente d'autres places
Que nous attendons encore ici-bas.
Agnès, je t'ai aimée à mon lever:
Fais qu'au coucher nous sachions nous trouver.

Charged

O cloud of passing glory, come again
To Tuscan hills, where still the vapours strong
Of youth's first bloom their freshness here regain
And tingle in the membranes where belong
The yesterdays we shared... Lost ecstasy!
O! lamb that I once loved, I have here found
The tremor of thy pulse! I see! I see!
I hear the echo of thy mystic sound:
Soft, gentle name that came and touched me deep
Within th'untouched recesses of a child,
Could I here ope these eyes and through them peep,
What seeing would I see 'mid rapture wild?
And what, fond Agnes, wouldst thou say to me
From 'yond the starry gaze of dazèd glee?

Montepulciano
(hearing of recent miracles)

42

Domine, labia mea aperies

When in the night we sing and sing again
Of what is here not seen, of what is not
Beheld or held in passing, when the pain
Of moments in obscurity forgot
Is heard upon the dark, and when the mark
Of Satan's passage o'er the soul of man,
That dandled o'er an æon in this dark,
Is felt where angels knelt as spectres wan
T'ward Hades' yawning jaw for aye and aye
At midnight's gong moved on with scarce a sigh,
When night is heavy, and the sound of day
For some is nevermore to hush this cry...
When, when, I say, a pause upon the world
Sends frissons through this earth, where mirth
seemed long
And night was spent in fondling, then is hurled
This gently turning ball 'neath our calm song
To vast Cacophony, to damnèd chords
Where one stilled Pendulum all beating hoards.

Ipsi peribunt, tu autem permanes
(Herculaneum*)

We have been here before, and there are days
That linger in the air and in the stone
That bear the prints of man, whose treading stays
Not long the launchèd rayon that we own
But for a summer's day, a yesteryear
That flickered for a while – we are not here
As long as long would seem, for very near
To hours long cast is this fast hour we steer.
O Yesterday! – the day we did believe,
The trouble far away, yet now to stay, –
Could we the sigh of seconds once more heave
And this the weight of moments weighed reweigh,
Would we await Tomorrow that may come
Or never come ere hours have sauntered home?

*Last seen in Classics student days, 1975.

Una messa mai finita

(Before the miracle, Lanciano)

Will this yet be, hid Lord, will this yet be?
The words sharp penned lest I be priested here,
The forces of this savage host set free,
The all of Hell let loose, will this yet hear
The sound of massive syllables anon
Pass o'er my head and through my idle tongue
Bid split the rocks of time and but in one
Short utt'rance glance through heavy æons long—
And bid Thee, Master, come and stand alone
Twixt heav'n and earth upon a moment small?
O Alpha and last Omega, dost own
The pow'r to crack the curse of Man, and call
From far Jerusalem, where beat this Heart
That, made of very flesh, tore sound apart?

Heart...: Science has discerned myochardial tissue.

Offeren nas gorffennwyd

(Y wyrth iwcharistaidd, Lanciano)

Pa beth yw hwn, Dduw gwyn, pa beth yw hwn,
Fod yma rywbeth mwy na'r hyn a'i deil?
O hen Fudandod maith, mi wn, mi wn
Mai distaw yw dy waith, dy iaith, lle gwneir
Y weithred eithaf, a'r ddieithraf un
A wnaed dan waedlyd rod: y Bod di-sail
A seiliodd yma'i dŷ, ac anwir lun
A guddia'r unig Wir a fu ddi-ffael.
O! Deyrnas gudd eonau, na fynn le
Ond rhwng briwsionyn gwan – O! fan rhy fawr
I engyl ac i ddyn, i ba ryw ne'
Yr af am air, am sillaf, am fer awr
O gysur rhwng y prysur oriau hyn
A oedodd unwaith daith un orig syn?

Pa beth...? – Adlais o eiriau San Rhisiart Gwyn, wrth iddo gael
ei greulon ferthyru.

(Ysgrifennwyd y soned tra y siaradai'r Prior â'r Archesgob.)

Ci sono troppe parole in giro per la casa

(Novice's comment regarding number of periodicals)

Enough, 'tis better than a heavy feast,
And many words that weigh upon the mind
That feeds upon the page – that rages least
In surfeit gorged when left a pause to find –
Are tasted less when wasted on the ear
Of th'inner man that can not walk alone
With but a slender sound, for found was here
No feeling felt, no feeling fully known.
O! tiny marks, wherein the spark of all
The pulse and impulse of convulsèd Sense
Walked on across the world, this tremored call
Of skull to hollowed skull through hollows dense
Was made to be but heard where't could be heard,
For echoes travelled ill a stillness stirred.

Oggi
("Beth yw ystyr Oggi?"*)

Tomorrow never was and never came
Across the patient skies, nor shall this day
Or hour or moment ever have a name
'Yond this that bids it be and holds its sway
Within the dangled æons that are not
Or ever were, save in a twinkle missed
By all that e'er it sought, for but a spot
Held all that shall through gyral orbs have hissed.
O! little dot, the plot of all the earth,
The house of human kind, the common place
Not treasured, for not measured for its worth! –
'Tween tap and tiny tapping, is there space
For all our morrows long, or is today
A hollow that tomorrow goes its way?

*My mother asked the meaning of the word.

48

Bernadette*
(Lk 13:30)

A little tremble that the world saw not,
A flicker in the dark it did not see,
A weak and frail fragility forgot,
Untouched, unnoticed by posterity
That gazed and gawked at greatness large and
loud
And worthy of all eyes – this wee thing
That never made a noise, this heavy shroud
Of nothingness all hid did nothing bring
To charm the planks and galleries of praise
Or soothe the pores that please – this tender beam
Ne'er shone upon a heart or thrilled the days
Of some enkindled tingle 'neath its gleam:
Thou wast and art unknown and shalt yet be
The last in worth, whom Earth passed utterly.

*A handicapped benefactress who spends hours
before the Blessed Sacrament.

Toi seul as compris
(Sister's farewell*)

 The soul of woman is not made of man,
Nor is the race that held him lightly weighed.
There is a myst'ry that hard calcule can
Not measure, where e'en Pleasure halts, afraid.
There is a space wherein my race moves not,
And hominides tread not the fairer land.
There is a knowing that the head forgot,
And pow'r to hold held by ne'er heavy hand.
And there is, barrèd heart, a part to play
Upon this planet's night that light ill caught,
For in the rayons passed 'yond noisome day,
There lingers some ray weak with contact fraught.
And, Anne, in these veiled eyes that gaze and gaze,
I see a look of looking of strange rays.

*She returns tomorrow to her enclosure.

Lift up þin herte unto God
wiþ a meek steryng of love

O God, upon the cloud I see Thee not,
And in the earth I hear not oft a sound
Of passing Trinity, and yet forgot
Was never yet a passage that I found
Upon a time where chimed the ages all
At treading of soft feet: a meeting was
Upon a molecule, and globules small
Did twinkle in the midst that Presence has.
O! ray of deeper dark! – There was a place,
And there is yet, where want can want no more;
There is upon this ancient stone a space
For two to lie where, trancèd here before,
The pilgrims of this darkened land did stand,
And for a moment held the Master's hand.

(In retreat, writing application
for perpetual vows)

Lift up...: From the anonymous *Cloud of Unknowing*, gift of Dr
James Hogg, friend and mentor, through whose provedential
guidance I'm making this application.

The clock

O little face, unconscious yet awake,
Tick on upon a plenitude of time,
And tick and tick again until it take
But yet another tap to make thee chime
The knell of all thy calling – call anon
Upon a soft oblivion, call the dream
Of this the morphined soul that lingers on,
And clap from slumber weighed th'alarmèd gleam.
O gong of sudden looking! – bliss and pain
Lie in the crack of ages in a sound
That came but one more time, that came again
And ne'er again, for, wound, 'twas hither bound
To tap no more the merriment of ease,
And moments travel far on ticks like these.

(In retreat)

Impegnato

A vessel is but filled when emptied all
And when alone all bare, for there is here
No room for two to be, and membranes small
That hide the busy soul move very near
To many worlds and galaxies of thought
That chance to travel by, and we are not
At home and fully there when elsewhere caught
In orbit wide, our little orb forgot.
O! many rays at wander, sunder this
Our pow'r to beam awhile, let us not stand
Too long where we belong, and bid us miss
The touch of something touching in this land
Where hurrying and worrying wear all
That rested ne'er 'tween rested membranes small.

(In retreat)

53

Vous avez été accepté
(à l'unanimité)

O! joy on earth! O! joy yet in the world!
To know that I am Thine, and Thine shall be,
And Thine alone, and by a little word
Upon this altar placed, eternally
To this Thy temple joined – to know that now
No man or angel fiend can mar the road
Trod here by friends now crowned, that once did bow
Here where I place my head: to see the cloud
Of witnesses unseen walk calmly by
And chuckle at an æon, to see all
Melt in a moment felt, nay, and to cry
A tear of blissful peace – this is to call
From out of the abyss of Failure vast,
And clutch at but a notch of grace at last.

> (I placed my head upon the high
> altar as the vote was being taken.)

Remote control
(«Vous avez sauvé ma vocation!»)

O! paix! O! paix! O! double paix profonde!
Parole dite, et vite proférée,
Son porté par le tremblement d'une onde
Muette, aveugle, mais transfigurée
Par ce rayon de sens, d'essence en feu
Qui sait trouver sa voix – Ô! grand Silence
De l'éternelle nuit, lueur d'un Dieu
Qui a tout dit en toute réticence...
Je vois, je crois, je prévois que demain
Est aujourd'hui écrit: Ta main reprend
Mes pas perdus, tient tous mes lendemains
Et sans grand bruit a tout dit, et comprend
Le sens de ce non-sens de ces faux pas
Ourdis sans ouï-dire d'Au-delà.

Ad Maiestatem

To love and be well loved, to be well known
Not by the ears of many and by all
That matter for a moment, but alone
To six that travel on a planet small
Called Solitude – to be no more than one
Forgotten in a band, to be a part
Of but a little land that this day's sun
Bid bind here ere the morrow's bid them part:
This is to shed a beam within a star
That will burn softly on, this is to be
A nought of nothing weighed where measures are
Held high upon the earth, high worth to see;
But this is to shine gently on and on
Upon a distant yesterday long gone.

(Feast of all our saints)

Præmonstratum*

(Written on the feast of the dedication of the Lateran basilica, after hearing a lady exclaim: «E' stupenda!» after entering our church.)

To build upon the earth a vault of heav'n
That will with glory beam, to hold a ray
Of God in stone well hewn and deftly giv'n
A light to tame, the ancient light to flay
In pore and prismic chis'lling – there to store
The trav'lling wave that left th'elysian home
Of soft Taboric ether where, before
The Light of light, the seraph eye did roam:
To come again, to come again, again
At clap of yestersound to crystal wall,
Jerusalem the blest, till tired stars wane,
And there upon the deep of Night to call –
This is to trap a glister in its flight,
To tune into a range of strange dark light.

*Recalling word of knowlege given previous autumn
(at Medugorje): "I see the door of a church opening."

Tabernaculum Altissimi
("Et ambulabunt mecum in albis.")

O! cell that never was and never came
To still the storm of age! O! page unwrit,
Unchiselled in the stone, that bore no name
Of sealed recluded soul... O! place unlit
By oil of midnight watching o'er the world...
O! silent land untrod, where God called not –
Or if He did, lost th'echo of His word –
O! bliss half-known, well-known and ne'er forgot:
I cannot hold my God within my home
Alone, alone, as utterly alone
As I had thought He'd bid, I cannot come
To knowledge of the One alone all known,
Unless it be in this the little wall
Of textile white wherein I now seal all.

Si solum fiat, sufficit*

("Magister, quare semper hoc loqueris?")

To live in love, to love, in love to be,
And to be nought but love – but to love well
With loving's art and skill: eternally
To be part of the loved, in Heav'n, in Hell,
And there for e'er upon a gaze to gaze
Unveiled in full at last, be't God or Fiend,
All seen beyond the screen of yonder days,
Seen in the visage 'hind which here 'twas
screened:
This is the all, this is the end of all
That matters in a day; there is no more,
No greater matter here: this measure small
Is all that shall weigh all, all evermore.
And simple, oddly simple words I hear,
As near as this my little brother here.

> *Words of the aged Apostle John, when
> asked why he always said the same thing.

Recevoir

There is but one, but one sole pow'r within
The soul of little Man; there is alone
'Mid wrestling brains one resting-place wherein
The moment may be spent and fully known;
There is but one small secret here on earth
By which the world is gained, by which the all
Of all that is may for its truer worth
Be measured and adored – one engine small –
And 'tis the wand that taps upon the land
Of magic moments made, of seconds weighed,
Of other moments marred or let to stand
Upon the shore of Possibles e'er laid:
'Tis this, the little bliss of knowing how
To touch but such alone as need be now.

(Christus Rex)

Silence

There is a hermitage upon the earth
Not made of brick or stone, nor of a seal
To bar a man from man; there is a hearth –
A shelter from the blast – that none may feel
Save such as there abide: a place to hide
Made of no matter dense, made full of Nought,
Made of a little space not very wide,
Yet locked by one great key all finely wrought.
There is, I do perceive, a place to be
Alone for ever, and all, all alone,
Where none again may roam, where none may
see
The inmate of a cell whose only stone
Is made of Will's command, that all may stand
Apart from but a magic of a land.

(Monte Oliveto)

Ausculta
(Benedictine retreat)

To listen is to look upon the soul,
To look and see, to gaze and softly gaze,
To hold a morsel and behold the whole
Whereof 'tis made, for oft the part betrays
The heart that bid it be: we are all seen
In this our naked walking in a word,
And in a sound is found where we have been,
For what was heard was ne'er again unheard.
Yet there is blindness in this little eye
That could behold the world, and there is more
That travels in the air than ear did spy,
For much did tap in vain at this clapped door.
There is a secret in the universe,
Yet few lips paused its lesson to rehearse.

"Flee. Keep silence. Rest."
(The three words heard by the great Arsenius)

There is too much to know, too much to brood
Upon this little globe; there is not here
A place to be, or space in Solitude
For distance from a memory too near;
There is in this long desert yet a throng
That has been here before, that will not go
As quickly as it came, for we belong
Within to th'inward land of all we know.
O! spectred strand of shadows, let me be
Alone with not a soul; let me be found
Tomorrow and tomorrow one day free
From days long gone and wraiths of lingered
sound.
O Master, let me nestle at this last
'Gainst Thee alone, till hours twice shown be
past.

Calm
(in retreat)

There is no need to talk upon a tone
Too high that it be heard: a word is not
A better for its din, nor do we own
The ear that turns away, for soon forgot
Was all not wanted well, was all that was
Not worth the pause that held it: none shall learn
A lesson yawned, and scorned is all that has
No spark to bid us mark a something burn.
We have heard all before, nor is there room
For sound in well bound knowledge: we know all
We need to know below, and none to whom
A word ungathered calls shall it recall.
And oft we trouble to shed louder light
That softer giving kept more dimly bright.

A second baptism

O Master, let me come and die at last
And on this altar bleed: this is the deed
That deadens every doubt, for here I cast
My anchor for all time, and this I read
On this high stone is shown to gazing eyes
That we see not, for angels here will land
To witness to this pledge, and in the skies
A copy of this writ will ever stand.
O Love of hidden pulling! I know ill
The shape of this long morrow, but I hold
The Hand that ever held it. Here I will,
I troth, I will my trothèd God enfold,
And do no more upon this Calvary
Than let it happen, let it, let it be.

(Last evening of retreat)

Writing perpetual vows

A little sheet that holds the living breath
Till it be breathed no more, a shape or two
That shapes a morrow wide, a mystic death
In testament here sealed, a moment true—'
Gainst which all Hell can clamour and e'er rack,
Should some hour cast it by—a handwrit pledge
Held by an unseen Finger that did lack
All means but one to keep me from love's edge.
O Love! I love Thee well, and could have loved
Another well indeed, for Thou dost know
The fondness in this glimmer, but where moved
The beck of this Thy shuffling that sighed, "No,"
Could I, sweet Lover of the heart so made,
Turn twice away from what long gazing bade?

Suscipe

O Master, this is all. I know that now
A word here heard was carried very far.
O King, I know in peace that where I bow
My head where Thou dost hide, nought now can mar
Again this hold of Godhead, that no face
Can shine or warm me ever but Thine own
Upon this land I tread, within this place,
This space that is the all that I shall own.
O Love that found the way, O Warmth that came
Between this gath'ring mist and gathered dark,
I heard this morn Thy whisper and my name
With Thine in wedlock sealed by but a mark.I heard,
my God, the morrow waiting here,
And in an echo Heaven very near.

(Alone, afterwards)

Absent

To mutter much, to utter much to men,
Nay, unto Thee as well to be too loud,
Is to be far from home, for no one then
Is here to hear Thee call, and I have bowed
Too often 'fore this Tent where blessings went
Another way for that the day was full
Of other noises made, of pulsings sent
Along these fibred passage-ways worn dull.
O! still small voice so often driven hence
And ne'er by membranes gathered—what are these
Hard twitchings of a mind and body tense
With massive meanings held, with words that please
Not well for too oft sent? Alas! We are
To pulses close but present from afar.

Διακονειν

(«Je vais voir l'Archevêque pour les
ordinations».)

O word of but a preacher, come again,
Not from the pen of etchings, but from this
The heart that heard the heart, that saw the pain
And softer joy within a sigh of bliss—
Come, comeand go across the rows of ears
That capture what moves here: go, go thy way
Into the breast that shed this night its tears
And to the brain that strayed this way this day.
Die, planted lie upon the morrow's thought,
And touch e'en such as came not hither well
To gaze at Beauty hid. Sound, dimly wrought
With syllables to steal a soul from Hell,
Be found tomorrow where a sorrow breaks
The heart cuirassed that heeds, and small heed
takes.

Beyond?

*(«Wer aber nicht glaubt, der wird ver-
dammt werden».*)*

What can I do, what can I do on earth,
That some may safely die? What may be done
Within a span of years, what deed of worth,
What moments bought and garnered ere be gone
The last that could aye stand, the one alone
That could for someone matter, that could buy
A hurried entrance there where some are shown
A door closed on a heavy, heavy sigh?
O Master, at the last what shall have been?
And could I stand already on that shore
Of minutes one time lent—could I the scene
Of Passing ever past see pass before
My ever fastened eyes—would I regret
A pain not gained for one not damnèd yet?

*Meditating on Mk 16:16, and
on the return of St Drithelm.

This is the day
(of return to Sélignac, 1976)

The sound of twenty twelvemonths in a day
Returns upon this hour, and vision strong
Beholds the mighty moments that now aye
Are buried in the dark that lingers long.
O! night of passing chances, evermore
In brightness hugely lit, what pain is this
That nothing can e'er mend? O! distant shore
Whereon a moment we did stand in bliss. ..
Why was this land so blessed so quickly cursed,
And for a sound of rhythmic tune e'er lost?
Had I one moment these long hours rehearsed
Ere on a morn the dawn of youth was tossed
Would yesterday have gone so calmly by,
Had it heard this tomorrow's heavy sigh?

Dom Damien

(of Sélignac, last recluse at Camaldoli)

To love too well a stone, to will to be
Within a place, a space well made, when bade
A Will another be; to will to see
No face but His alone, to lie e'er laid,
Recluded by the tomb of high disdain
And higher height of praise; to be well known
And shown to all and sundry; to refrain
From all but limelight gawked and basked alone:
'Twere to be well paid here, and there, beyond,
Where Thou dost wait awhile and calmly smile
At hominides' fond play, made doubly fond
By this its bliss of preening in fair style—
My God, 'tis to want more than what Thou art,
For Thou'dst have nought here wrought of glory's art.

Domine, quid me vis facere?

O! calm of utter loving!—I know not
The morrow's form or yesterday's fond dream,
What meaning it may have, e'en though forgot
Was ne'er the beauty of this little gleam
Seen once upon the night, the lamp alight
Hard by the Tent of Godhead, where all slept
But Prayer alone awake, all, all still bright
In soft recluded burning hourly kept:
There is no sign or writing on this wall
Of waiting in the dark, no God-writ mark
But this, O silent Master, this one call
That none but this mine angel shall remark.
For two have placed a mark upon this stone,
And Thou'dst have done but what one stroke hath
shown

How beautiful are the feet
of those who bear good tidings
(«C'est un des jours les plus heureux de ma vie!»*

O! bliss in but a sound! O! happy day,
That changes every day for evermore,
That brings back yesterday from far away,
And sparkles with a grace once known before!
A word this hour was heard that has a pow'r
Beyond the noise of scribblings and of hands
Not driven from above; nay, one small hour
O'er years of heavy waiting calmly stands.
My God, I shall Thee touch, I shall Thee hold,
And be Thy voice on earth—I shall be free
To climb these ancient steps and there be bold
To walk alone 'mid clouded Trinity.
I shall, hid Friend, for ever and a day,
A Priest be, till the æons fade away.

*Written after Fr Prior's talk with the Archbishop.

How sweet the sound of a sound can be...

O! joie profonde! O! belle et douce extase
Inconnue de ce monde—inconnue, oui,
D'hier, d'avant-hier. .. O! douce phrase
Portée à mes oreilles aujourd'hui,
Proférée par les siècles dès l'aurore
De l'univers en feu—O! son d'un Dieu
Éloigné et si proche!. .. Approche, adore,
Bon ange, compagnon de ce saint lieu!—
Demain nos mains Le toucheront, nos voix
Le créeront, ce Maître-Créateur,
Qui créa ce frisson, ce mot d'un choix,
Court Oui immense et dense de lueur,
Qui brilla dans l'obsurité profonde,
Que pénétra le tremblement d'une onde.

We are what we were

There is a sadness in the universe
That yawns a heavy pain: there is a sigh,
A melancholy meant for ne'er a verse
And piercèd by no pen, for moments high
With pressure doubly pressed can linger on
Long after they have been, and we have seen
The mighty deeds of mischief chiefly done
When they had ceased to be what once had been.
O sounds of double pricking, come again
And gain your lasting home within this land
Of Thought and Mem'ry dense, and leave your pain
A little longer where no stronger hand
Could come and lift your plague, for nothing more
Than Yesterday has pow'r o'er Evermore.

4/1/97

Reduce, Reduce
(Portio mea Dominus)

And yet there is a joy in little things
Where brims a distant Light: there is a place
Where sound in silence sweet yet softly sings
And where a presence dense yet moves apace
And taps us homeward-bound—there is an hour
Wherein the hours are still and will not be
As hurried in their chime; there is yet pow'r
Within a sound to bid us all things see.
And there is, ancient Peace, a place for Thee
When less is done on earth, when worth is not
Alone in great noise prized, for only he
Found all on earth that settled on his lot.
And many joys were missed for greater bliss
That never was, for 'twas not without this.

We're coming
(Ellen's recorded message)

The engines of the mastered mind of man,
The craft of holding all and calling on
From absent Being where no meaning can
Across the waters march—the dabblings done
To voices never heard, to sounds encased
In boxes technic and compressions pressed
There where no limb may meet or gazing chaste
May mingle eye with eye in fondled rest:
These are the pains of molecules that move
Upon a chordless lyre, yet these are fire
Ignited unbeknown to frigid groove
And kilometric sound all bound awire.
Yet in a dormant echo there is more
Than oft a frequent frequency before.

Open

O mystery! O secrecy unveiled!
This is the all of all; this is the spot
Whence hangs the universe; here unassailed
The moments ever are: 'tis this the lot
Giv'n but to very few, for few e'er knew
The secret of it all, and Yesterday
Tomorrow would have taught this something new
And very very old, giv'n but a way.
'Tis naught but th'art of parting with this key
Upon the moment held, the holding here
The mastery of hours, the pow'r to be
What, where, and how we'd be, the vision clear
That ne'er would know a cloud, for he alone
That chose no more to choose did aught e'er own.

Dyma fan yn ymyl Duwdod

O! fendith yn y pridd ac yn y tir
Lle troediodd llawer un! O! fan rhy fawr
I enaid un neu ddau! O! ddyddiau hir
Yr oesau a fu gynt! O! gyson awr
Yr hen atalnod llawn, lle'r awn yn ôl
I'r echdoe pellaf un, sy'n oedi dro
Rhwng brys a rhuthr rhawd a red yn ffôl
O afael hyn o heddiw sydd ar ffo—
O! orig hen, dan wên eonau'n bod
Fel 'roeddynt ryw bell ddoe, ryw well fwyn ddydd,
Tyrd, oeda yma awr, awr henaidd glod
Yr Hen Ddihenydd maith yfory fydd
Yn disgwyl eto'r oed, yn troedio'n bell
Ac agos, agos iawn hen barth sydd well.

Plume

Ô voix silencieuse, toi, demain,
Vas rester ici-bas, et seul le son
Qui sort et sortira de cette main
Parcourra ces beaux champs d'Elysion
Qui taisent tout parler. .. Reparle, et sois,
Amie de solitude, le témoin
Des courants intérieurs, lesquels, parfois,
Se servent de ton fil pour aller loin.
Ô petit rien de rien, qui relies tout—
Qui relira ta trace—ô face enfin
Dévoilée quand le voile et le long clou
Du sort aura scellé ce court Destin,
Sauras-tu dire avec ta faible voix
Une étincelle éteinte, qui fut moi?

(Veille de la Sainte-Agnès)

Calamus scribæ

O mouth that never spoke, and taught the world,
Unvibrant voice where trembles evermore
The laden line wherein lies but a word
From mind to mind e'er sent—O! cry of yore
That dwindled not as quickly as the night
Where twinkled soft a spark—how oft a mark
Did carry ancient seconds into sight
And palp again the corners of the night. ..
Calm tracèd blue, lost hue of yesterday
On calmer white left here, let here to be
The chargèd current where again draws nigh
The moment felt through this capillary—
O ear that listened ne'er, yet caught it all,
Lie, sleep upon this sheet, and æons call.

(St Agnes)

Beside the Syrian sea

A little touch, a little, little word
That echoed through the heavens and called down
The ancient Voice of all—my Lord, 'twas heard,
The whisper on the deep, and this the gown
To prophets of the word was giv'n before,
For still the still small spirit is abroad
And hands have handed on a touch of yore
That came from yonder stars poised here-toward.
O! tingle of all ages, passing through
The christic fingers small: the calling days
Of Galilee 'cross skies of Tuscan hue
Have dawned, and 'tis the moment of strange rays. ..
O! mark and seal of Godhead on the soul!
This is the part long wanted–'tis the whole.

Tears

("I cried throughout the whole ceremony."*)

A droplet is a molten part of man
And woman kind all felt, a globule small
Of utterness all held, where utt'rance can
No more its meaning send, an end of all
That was e'er left unsaid, a bleeding deep
Where fest'rings poured through pores pressed open wide
A gate that at an utmost could not keep
The most of all, the swollen heavy tide.
There is a language in a molecule
Of blended sadness made, whereof the ear
The grammar learned not well: a little pool
As old as oldest man, a silent tear
Held louder sense than denser meanings far,
And we are very liquid when we are.

*Ellen's words

84

Unknown secret

(il quadro misterioso)

There lie upon a canvas many years
That travelled never on, while onward went
The moments where they were, and many tears
Once shed one yesterday were never meant
For this the morrow's ears, for we walk not
With sharpened sense well tuned to what has been,
And what hurt much awhile was soon forgot,
For we know not what never we have seen.
Yet in a face long frigid some may see
At whiles a smile that was, and there shines yet
'Tween molecules long stilled eternity
In moments caught, in painted droplets wet.
For tears came once this way, but did not stay,
Unless it be in this that sighs for aye.

(All'Apparita, casa del Dott. Giovanni Guiso)

Hit

(by Alessandro's Ordination gift*)

There is a button that can move the world
Within, within, where we have walked before,
And on this respun band all sounds are hurled
To caverns deep that yet keep safe the store
Of days forgot: we are not safe with this
Small magic ribbon vast, where cast is all
The spell of scented hell and rewept bliss,
For naught as sound twice caught has pow'r to call.
O! music of my yesterday!—I hear
The voices and the dreams that once walked by,
And though I mingle with what here draws near,
I cannot o'er long sorrow too long sigh,
For homeward now I know I am here bound,
And I hear music at the end of sound.

*Simon and Garfunkel: *Greatest Hits.*

86

Çome tu sei fui ancor io:
Com' io sono sarai ancor tu.
(Skull at old hospital in Siena)

O part of man, whole of humanity,
That smiles and waits a little while for us
That look not where we go—Eternity
In but a moment's rest, a globule thus
Of matter chatt'ring not where sound can hear,
All of a gaping hole that whole books writes
And reads again where chapters lived are near
For ever, ever more 'neath truth's great lights:
O time in but a fraction, breaking all
That ever came this way, time standing long
Upon a skull long emptied, yawn the call
Of all that for a moment here belong:
Grin placidly there where the din is gone
From this wide jaw that æons belched or won.

Cronaca
(daily responsibility)

We trace the line of moments on a page
That will to yellow turn and leave behind
All trace but this of them that came of age
And yielded unto seconds—this, the mind
And minding well of wriggles that hold all
The meaning of a day, this little brain
Of mem'ry marked and coded, this faint call
Of nothings ever wrought will call again,
Again, again, again when we have gone,
But none will turn to listen to a sound
Of matter made of nought, for we have done
Today as yesterday as we were bound,
And morrows have a pattern that we know,
And there is little here the truth to show.

De cella in cælum
(construction of new cell)

A corner of the cosmos, but a space
Wherein till death to hide, nay, not too wide
But wide enough for Godhead—one last space
Wherein vast æons march, a cell beside
The lamp where burns my Lord, a little spot
That none on earth shall see, where none may come
To strange an exile hearth, where are forgot
The sounds of yesterday, the sounds of home:
This is a-building here, and years stand long
'Tween these new-standing walls, where evermore
The hours will swing 'twixt syllables and song,
For all to be must be 'hind this one door.
O! home hard by my Home, come now and be
A dungeon barred enough to set me free.

A friend

We travel on a lonely homeward road
Upon this empty globe, where many men
Walk far and wide 'side home and sealed abode
That others may not tread: a hovelled den
Away, away from all is all I see
On this idyllic land, where stand well grasped
The châteaux and the palaces of glee
That dreams knew well to buy and wallets clasped.
Yet there are moments when a little gleam
Made all of looking well have held a home
Not of hard mortar struck, but of a dream
Of being bold, of being told to come
And hide a little in a shelter frail
That, made of nothing, did in nothing fail.

Curriculum vitæ

Abbiamo qualch'istante qui, lo so,
E qualche giorno di serenità:
Il paradiso del diacono
È corto, e la lunga verità
Del tempo rivenuto mai sarà
La sola che rimanga: mai, mai più
Vedremo questa pace—e ci verrà
La lunga sera della gioventù.
O! gioia dell'Altare, data qui
All'alba della vita, sarai-tu
Memoria domani solo—sì,
E sogno, sola verità quaggiù?
Quest'oggi dammi bere, vivere:
Il sogno forse è più dell'essere.

Media vita in morte sumus

(sung at Compline at this time)

When we have travelled on, and moved afar
Upon the dawns that wake us, take us there
Where all things have their rest, when this our star
That glimmers through our morn has bid us wear
Our solemn even's robe, and we no more
Have time to rhyme or riddle with our fate,
But stand with understanding at the door
To which none came that hasted or was late,
What will the droplet of a beam of time
That we to ink did dye seem then, and then
How will the sound of this once well wound chime
Rebound across the closing ages' glen?
And will there be an hour to look again
And wish, half-wish, we could one hour yet gain?

When there is not a moment yet on earth
That will be ours again, when gain is not
In merriment or moments of high mirth
Known to have been, and when the measured lot
Of seconds tapped has tipped into our lap
And we have heard the word that utters all,
For that no more is said, will one last tap
As soft as any other be our call,
And will tomorrow hold our yesterday
Well poised beneath its gaze? Will there be none
To whisper, "Come again! We'll come away
To paths long trod, to actions long, long done."?

For we have sinned a little upon earth,
And damnèd æons clasped a little mirth.

Or will we be upon the isle of doom
A little brighter in our homeward gaze?
The hollow of this passage-way to gloom,
Will't shed a glister on our unmapped days?
And will the stretching of our utmost yawn
Bring sleep too heavy for our crinkled smile?
Will this the hap and scheming of our dawn
There seen again, bring pain or rest awhile?
Will we have been, when we can be no more,
And these the happy moments that we were
To be, one day to be, when nevermore
They can e'er chance to be, will they be there
Upon the cosmos standing, to end all
That never shall have been, by one stroke's call?

Reading lines penned beside
Dom Damien's tomb
*(while praying intensely at Camaldoli
at this time of year, 1985)*

And yet when in the heart the word returns
That came this way before, and when the door
That was not taken well—though heavy yearns
Did sigh to have it pushed—stands evermore-
Untapped, unconquered o'er the passing years,
Then, hid Delight, hid in the night that was,
There comes a burning made of heated tears
For what may never be what one life has,
For we are moving on, and days decline
More quickly than their morn, and we are not,
'Neath vows well made, e'en though each fibre Thine,
As free to see and choose our portion's lot,
For we are masters over but an hour,
And o'er all æons more have little pow'r.

(St Colette)

Haunted

(by Julian, Colette*, Romuald,
Sr Nazarena. ..)

O! Damien, O! Colette, this heavy day
Is laden with much barring e'ermore barred
From one life's grasp: this safe and fencèd way
That could have been so fond, Time's wand it marred
By but a little tapping—Nazarene,
And Julian, my own Julian, my long friend,
Whose visage veiled and glory hailed unseen
Shone with me in the cell till Youth's blitzed end—
I cannot be so far from where you were,
From where we were together: there is more
To grace once giv'n than faces that did stir
Awhile the heart of man—this once sealed door
At which I stood and looked will stand again,
And I can not live long 'neath this look's strain.

*6/3

95

After Communion
(as deacon at High Mass)

There is, my Lord, a word, a secret sound,
Known unto those alone that know Thee well—
A gentle tone, a meaning where is found
The sense that was not touched, that none did tell,
For that 'twas never told: to hold a light
No syllable did serve, when truth like this
Came loudly through the ear, not uttered quite
But felt as e'er was felt the softest kiss.
For time is short on earth, and this, my Guest,
This day for evermore Thou'dst have me know,
For 'tis a secret at the which a rest
Is offered unto one that knew not how
To bear the weight of never having been
What he had wanted well, what he had seen.

Tis this, my loving Lord, 'tis this alone,
This little flickered light, this might not made
Of much, but of a touch but touched and known,
A coming near of nought but thought unweighed,
Unnoticed and ungrasped where rasping sounds
Did dull the fullest sense, the sense of all
That ever had a name, for there resounds
Upon the universe a converse small:
Tis this, hid Lord; 'tis this, hid God, whose word
I heard within the cup, whereon there lay
A legion of soft wings; 'tis this, where stirred
The cosmos that I held, for Thou didst say
A word I heard where ne'er an ear could move:
Nay, 'tis enough. It is enough to love.

A given time

(after Fr Prior's announcement*
in Chapter)

A date is but a dot upon the map
Of plotted seconds' course, a *when* to be
Some moment known, another little tap
'Tween tappings without end, eternity
Unique in that it came, in that it struck
This one and only shape that will remain,
And though the ramblings of stray chance and luck
May foul e'en yet, a date doth fate retain.
It is too long; tomorrow will not come—
Nay, nay, it never came; it never was,
For ever morrow was a bliss for some
In their afar off wanting, yet it has
A strange, strange way of coming nigh
When, only when, we for it no more sigh.

*La tua ordinazione sarà ...
la vigilia di Tutti i Santi.

IHS

heri, hodie, et semper

A stone is but a molecule or two
Of matter duly made and left to stand
Where it must long remain, yet through and through
I know a mystery within this land
Of history well set, where yet the soul
Of yester sacred day walks strongly on,
And in this brittle part there domes the whole
Of glory's blazèd trail where sparkles shone.
O shreds of Godhead trailing yet awhile
In corpulets so fine, divine ye are,
Beyond this crystal light, where file on file
Of spectred lined battalions travel far
Into a distance that no eye can see,
Into a music carved of ecstasy.

(Rome)

A yearn

Will this yet be? Will this yet come again?
Will yesterday yet dawn and bring us home
To joy long gone, that days could not contain,
For that they had an end and did once come
Too often where we were, where we were well,
Too well, to be well long, for we were not
Made to be always well where lingers hell
'Mid moments that we tread 'neath our dread lot. ..
O! yet, I hear it come, I hear the day
That will not come again perhaps bid be
A word that, heard, has pow'r to bear away
A mighty weight of missing: this I see
I can see for a little while yet here,
If but a syllable bring old dreams near.

(Rome)

Madonnina
(Civitavecchia)

O! sangue dell'Amore—sangue che
Ci parla senza suono: voce mai
Sentita ne udita qui—perché
Venir in questa notte, che ormai
Sorriderà dell'ingenuità
D'infanti creduli, perché dirai
Parole oggi dall'eternità?
O! Cuore che ci porta! Grida qui
L'inferno di domani: oggi fa'
Soltanto una lacrima per chi
Non sa più piangere nell'Aldilà.
Silenzio!—dell'anima che sa,
Sa tutto, nell'istante che sarà. ..

Politesse

To talk across is never to be heard,
In that we would not listen–'tis to be
Of little worth in uttering a word
Awaited not and weighted not, but free
And easy in its coming, coming oft,
Too oft for laden ears; for sounds, like tears,
Are gathered best where rest is very soft,
And deaf proximity no being nears.
O! angel that spoke well in Galilee
On bended knee at Womanhood all low,
A highest seraph in a courtesy,
All ear for but a whisper, but a bow:
Teach us to tremble at a tremored space
Of air on fire where soul a soul can face.

Quam terriblis est locus iste

Ne pas y arriver, ne pas s'y faire
Mais piétiner longuement et, pire,
Reculer en chemin, et puis défaire
Le bien qui fut fait—mon Dieu, et dire,
En faisant ce grand rien, que je suis
Élu, voulu pour Toi, Toi seul; que Toi,
Tu voulais tout donner, pardonner, puis
Ordonner en bon ange pour son Roi. ..
Ô Maître! je T'ai aimé, et j'ai su
Que Tu m'aimais encor, qu'encor Tes yeux
Me voulaient près de Toi—Shaddai, j'ai vu
Ta main qui me créa, et sous Tes cieux
D'orage je T'ai touché en ce lieu
Baigné de sang, baigné d'amour en feu.

**Rühme dich nicht des morgigen Tages;denn
du weißt nicht, was der Tag bringt.**
(Pr 27:1)

What will the morrow bring? What will the day
Be at its ever ending? What are these
Tomorrows that I see and will, as they
Now stand, e'en so to be, e'n so to please?
And yesterday that was, that now no more
Is here, yet here is ever and remains
Far fonder than today, with hours of yore
Too bright in mem'ry's sight that colour gains—
Is this the all of living, being all
But where alone to be we are but bound,
And is there ever hour that can but call
And bid us rest therein and 'neath its sound
Of calmly tapping measure calmly wait
For but a pleasure of a pulse's weight?

Apology for Poesie

(La poésie, comme la prière, est une échelle vers le ciel.)*

O instrument of gold, as old as all
The tools of well trained man—O stain of sound
Reheard within capillaries that call
From brains and neurons by a small shape bound
An ancient patient word to pick again
From its long dormant lying—little line
Above, below now falling 'neath the strain
Of meaning thinly held, two days entwine:
The thought of one lost moment ling'ring e'er
In th'air above this page all age withstands,
And music made of syllables two share
Through one frail slender trail that joins two lands.
Soft palpitated Sense, sense, palp the years
For some with feeling eyes, and looking ears.

*Virgil Gheorghiu. (Cf Sir Philip Sidney.)

O! cell
(in memory's cells beheld)

To think and think again upon a while
That will not come again, for that it was
Once only near at hand; to watch the smile
Of yesterhour that stands where nothing has
The pow'r again to be; to see the all
In but a part now lie, there where we are
Ne'ermore to tread, and there for e'er to call
Across the placid æons from afar:
This is to be today far, far away
From what awhile we had, for sadness great
Can stand in memory, and but a day
That mattered not, that thought not long to stay,
Can linger evermore where we belong,
For 'tis to hurt for e'er to have done wrong.

Familiar

I will return again upon a day
Thine own to own—O Master! I will come
If Thou wilt have me there, if Thou wilt say
In peace, "Let peace return. Let peace be home!"
O solitude! The name, the well known sound
Of silence 'tween hard walls!. .. There calls again
A mighty weight of Hiraeth where redound
The doubly emptied spaces of fond pain.
I cannot be, my God, I cannot be
Alone too long with others: other men
Tread oft where soft Thy rising I could see
When dawn was still, when all was still, and when
The stillness of the all was all I knew,
And emptiness was space enough for two.

(Easter Monday, "a great while before dawn")

Amazed

(to discover the date*)

Is there an accident or dent in Time
Not bent ere ages were? Is there a day
That happens here to come and calmly chime
Its passage through our sky, that stood not aye
Upon the archives written where we are
Already seen and heard? Is there a word,
A moment, but a moment, 'neath our star
That æons measured not long ere we stirred?
And, Wolfgang, is it naught but wind and air
That blows our blessing hither? Is this mark
That from the heights will come, fraught with the glare
Of Turin's ancient gleam, but digit stark
On signed chronometry pushed by a pen,
Or was a hand well handling little men?

*St Wolfgang's intercession had been
especially sought, at his tomb.

Quite amazed

(by Turin fireman's report)

When news is long in coming, and stale facts
At last can blast the cloister, what are these
Large eyeballs made to see 'mid frigid acts
Of calm collected writing—histories
Of human moves all made, weighed by the line
Of Reason's placid smile: what noise of day
Lies buried on the page, where markings fine
Mark traces of a God upon our way?
O! testimony of a common man
That climbed to save his King, what thing is this
That shoved thy frightened leaping as none can
Push, pull or tap in time—for time to miss
Was none where burned the singeing of our hours
In raiment meant to stand all cosmic pow'rs.

Custos, quid de nocte?
Custos, quid de nocte?

The night is made of knowing, hearing well
And seeing all that moves upon the dark
Collected moments that all moments tell
Whereof they could be made—for but a spark
Made of a night that was is all we are
And evermore shall be when earth's long sleep
Has bid us take our rest where dreams afar
In regions blest or damned long vigil keep. ..
O! land of well lit gazing, where the eye
Views all 'neath fastened lids and fastest hold
Of vision doubly dark: the noon-day sky
Has not a ray as bright, or sight as bold
As this the stillness of a clarity
That sundered oft a coughed eternity.

Sunt lacrimæ rerum

O! goodness undefiled, unanswered, e'er
Uncaptured and uncaught where gleams walk on
Without a pulse to follow—ever there
And burning softly with the beams that shone
For ne'er a man, unless it be for one
That heard what thou didst offer, offered not
And offer never wouldst till days had done
Their greying work to this thy cast off lot.
O! angel, I knew well what thou didst say
In saying ne'er a word, in saying all
In droplets held no more from light of day,
For 'twas the day that ratified thy call:
The voice of Godhead passed, sweet soul, through thee,
That mattered not to none, that none did see.

13–14/4

(midnight)

Negli occhi
(d'un quadro—dell'Arcivescovo)

To know, good Lord, that we shall yet embrace,
That we shall touch and, touching, look and look,
And, looking, see and see, nay, that the Face
That beamed into my soul at th'hour it took
Its leave of uncleft void, will gaze anon
Into its firmest depth and fairly blaze
Its former shrouded gaze for e'er upon
A whole of singèd soul for unseen days—
Not on the shore of æons, far away
From Time's momentous hold upon our land,
But on a day our own, a little day
That has been marked by but a touch of hand
That labours 'neath a load of cosmic rays:
This is to sigh where Godhead man obeys.

Résonances

O little light upon the Godhead waiting,
Watching o'er hours that think not of their King,
Teach me to ponder on the world's long wasting
Of this old spark, that wakened everything.

O darkened land, where stood 'tween age and morrows
Angels and fiends, where beams of light hard die,
Here in the night the might of distant sorrows
Travels again the pain of some hid sigh.

Somewhere alone a heart knows well its burden,
Turning while burning this plays softly on:
There in the stillness of the land untrodden
Some breast unheard well veils a beauty shone.

Sorrow is long where long was one in coming
That in a look took Yesterday away,
And in this night yet oft a spirit roaming
Travels alone toward another day.

And day brings not a morn where dawns a glory
Made of a ray that but another sent:
Day led to day that ended daylight's story
For oft a heart that heard what evening meant.

Lord, I have known and heard this night the meaning
Of but a word ill-heard but shyly writ,
And in a look of eyes, seen angels gleaning
What never was, where't beamed where all was lit.

Friends of an hour, the pow'r of this your glowing
There where we are, ere daylight dulls the ear,
Calls from afar, yet there is in your growing
One day too oft, a soft and twice shed tear.

(Tune: *Hedd)*

A syllable of power
(on the Prior's lips)

O joy! O utter joy! A day will come
When I shall hold Thee high there where once trod
The feet of dreaming youth, and, coming home
To this Eternal City where my God
Lives on 'mid spurnèd grace and spawnèd sin,
Will these old yellowed leaves once more peruse
And use the cells of Intellect within
To spy a land too fair e'en for the muse. ..
Aha! my Lord, this word heard in the e'en
Hath held a happy evening and a dawn
That I had long, long hoped and never seen,
For that the morrow's veil seemed ever drawn.
But doctored shall it be by ecstasy
Of but a simple bliss . . .

                    −enough for me.

First sacrament

O little child, whom here we consecrate,
Wilt thou tomorrow be a child of Hell,
Or will the magic rays that emanate
From this Siloam come and, at thy knell,
Bid æons halt, to let thee enter in
To where by right, by rite, thou dost belong
'Mid other angel wings? Nay, chainèd Sin
Here snapped, will it for aye repeat earth's song:
Will Adam live again, and pain long gone,
Will't be the lot of yet a little soul,
And this great mark and question that here shone
Upon this blessèd head, will it the whole
Of myriad moments blast when 'tis too late,
Or will a little water demons sate?

Waiting

To wait is to be empty for a while,
To linger and to hunger ere it come,
To be today beneath tomorrow's smile,
At home in th'antechamber of our Home:
To be with Naught well filled, and to be stilled
By happ'nings coming not, to be made well
By will and Will well wed where all is willed
In confines of this hour—'tis this to tell
The meaning of it all, here where we are
Upon the world's lashed shore, with nothing more
Than loving to be done. For much can mar
The little that need be, and when 'tis o'er,
The tapping of this hand, the land we tread
Will calmly wait again for days unsaid.

Ἁρμονία

My soul has seen a secret, and my cell
Has held the light withheld from dazzled eye
And pulsed and pounded ear, for here to dwell
Is to be heard and known beneath the sky
By none of human kin, to win no heart
Or thought by other shared, but to belong
Unto the long Amen and here to part
With but a fading echo of a song.
O! music of the æons! I have found
Alone the all of all, and it is this
The very fondling of a tender sound
Made all of stray meanders of a bliss.
For e'en the spheres can dance upon a line,
And but a pause can cause a trance of Thine.

A child
(that has no television)

A child is but a wilder moment, not
E'er meant to linger long, a song that was
Not heard while yet 'twas sung, a day forgot,
For that 'twould come again. And come it has
Till it has ever gone, and gone for aye
As aye can only be, for evermore,
For ever was ne'er longer than a day
That in an oft soft falling æons saw.
And yet a child that smiled for but an hour
Upon an ageing noon—that looked and heard,
That hung not on electrons, and had pow'r
To stand alone and utter her own word—
Can send a twinkle yet that will not end
As soon as belchèd ions that beards tend.

(Orsa, the child of Ornella and Léonel Cousin,
at the remote country house of Centini)

Blitzed
(by a loaded cassette*)

There are some mighty pulses that the ear
Holds not as well as th'air; there throbs within
The banks of mem'ry's cells a shock to tear
The hardest stoic wall, and but a din
Made of a long lost rhythm, that had been
Held by the spark of growing that we were,
Can stir too many yesterdays once seen,
For sounds are clad again as they were there.
O! voices of my youth, what truth are you,
So far and so well known—what heavy joy
Made all of wanting more here passes through
Your real presence dense? O! harmless toy,
That crammed the damnèd hours into a band,
I hear too much to touch in peace thy land.

*Of pirated Beatle sounds

The fairest Mass on earth

O! Beauty doubly blest, where rests the King
Upon a ray His own—O! sound of Home
Made of the magic columns that here sing
'Tween pipes so huge and small, and that but come
Upon the air vibrated that we move
With mastered voice and hand: O! land where tread
Anon the feet of angels . . . nay, no groove
Or stored trick all electric did the dead
Awake from their long slumber as did this
The mischief of a molecule or two
That hid the Godhead's trick'ry—this the bliss
Contained where is retained what once we knew
Ere e'er we came to be, for we were there
Within the Master's thinking on the fair.

Cyffur yn yr awyr

*(wrth i'r clychau seinio eto,
adeg y Pedwar Amser)*

O! gân yr hen ganrifoedd yn y gwynt
A ddeil acenion doe ac echdoe hir
Y flwyddyn ddaw yn ôl ar gyson hynt
Yr atalnodau hyn—O! sain y Gwir
Nas cyfnewidir chwaith, O! faith fwyn gân
A glywir eto lle daw engyl lu
I gyffwrdd â'n diarffordd nodau mân
A gyfyd gyda'r wawr a'r awr a fu:
Tyrd, hedd a hud yr oesau yn dy ôl
I'r parthau hyn, a boed i darth a swyn
Aroglau'r weddi hen, eithafoedd ffôl
Y caru sydd rhy gryf i'r eithaf ddwyn,
Cans yma'r ŷm lle buom ni o'r blaen,
Ac y mae llawer haen dan dawel faen.

Tutto, ma tutto
(Clementina, 22 anni)

O hidden breast, caressed by not a touch
Of soft created hand, but handled all
By fire unseen, by fondling that was such
As eye saw not on earth, for one gaze small
Looked through thy darkened night and saw thee well,
Too well to tell the tale, for told was not
The heaviness of heaven and of hell
That struggled for a little hug forgot:
Forgotten shalt thou lie upon the dark
Of this thy morrow long, where song shall be
Not music made the melody to mark
Of youth's full opened mirth, but ecstasy
All of a blending made to end it all,
All, all, I say, in this veiled wedding call.

(At midnight. Cf Mt 25:6)

"I will always be there for you."

A heart that beats apart from all that know
And see with but the eye, a sigh of peace—
And not for grasping sent,—a distant glow,
A flame upon the night that will not cease:
O! gift and boon of Godhead fully wed
To Manhood's soul spread o'er an altar vast,
This is, I see, the end of all e'er said
'Tween word and meaning 'cross the skyline cast.
O Ellen all alone upon an hour
Of growing unto age, a page holds well
The silence slightly broke by gentle pow'r
Of ink that twinkles softly here to tell
What never shall have been when we have gone,
What no man shall have seen that untouched shone.

Omne donum perfectum

And yet upon the night there is a light
That will not go away, for stay I will,
Sweet soul, with this thy shining, for the sight
Of being is not seen, but in the still
And calm of hearing all, the smallest word
Can hold a long beholding, and the eye
And ear need here not feed on senses heard,
For much can travel from a silent sky.
And I have known upon a little sheet
A fondle made of nought but what we are,
For in a world of jabbing, meaning sweet
Can stroke a broken heart from very far.
And there is yet a morrow here today,
For cosmic void has room for one weak ray.

What is this life?
(J'ai gaspillé ma vie à faire trop de choses...*)

There is too much to do on earth, and more
Than need be done is done by all that do
Too much to do all well, for this one law
Of patient moments old, that ancients knew,
The new-found sound of man can ill contain,
And waning is the moon that should have known
To slowly be, to wholly be again
What once it calmly was to days outblown.
O Master of the energies of flesh,
That twitch and chatter o'er a loudest day
That held a bulging load, what did enmesh
The very brain that breathed, till it should pay
A debt too heavy to a great machine
That had no pow'r to stop till all had been?

*Paroles d'un Chartreux.

The tourists

("All the lonely people . . .
. . . No one was saved.")

As lonely as a crowd, among a throng
That moves and mumbles and goes on its way
Into the long unknown, each bathed in song
Magnetic for a pause at heat of day,
Clad well in Hell's attire, all wired for Sin
In raiment not much worn, and torn apart
Not much from clutches firm and morphined din
That nursed the deadened paddings of the heart:
The folly fouls the sound of this fair place,
And where at night we sing there clings a curse
To hurried feet, to face on worried face
That must see in a day the universe . .

Yet there is oft awhile in some stray eye
That looked and looked again for something more
Than meddling upon earth, a distant sky
Of thoughts unheard, unknown, for 'hind this door
Of lonesome human kind a cosmos whole
Is dandled o'er a little damnèd soul.

First Matrimony

A life, two lives, lives yet to be, can lie
Upon a sound here uttered: evermore
The will's consenting word the world doth tie
To this one bond of two, and 'tis the store
Of but a couple's little universe
That fastens this small ring to this small hand
That was by fondling held for better, worse
And worst of all to be, should this fair land,
The paradise of mornings yet unborn,
Tomorrow and tomorrow souring learn.
O! merriness of moments all unworn,
What will the freshness find when age shall burn
A little more than needed this first flame
That could upon a wrinkle shine the same?

Letter to a friend

(P. Winfried, Camaldolese,
on the feast of Saint Romuald)*

I hear upon the night a lonesome day
That Company knew well, I hear the pain
Of what no more shall be, for gone away
Is now the bliss of sorrow stroked again.
O! cell that held the universe at bay,
Yet held enough for loving, loving all
That need be held on earth, O! hour astray
That took from hours e'ermore the fairest call—
I cannot be, I cannot be again
What solely I can be; there is no room
Within the cosmos left where yet to own
A corner of a glory from the gloom.
It is too late, nor ever shall there be
A space again made wide enough for Thee.

*Written after preaching on the succession
of recluses ,including Dom Damien, Sr Nazarena. ..

BBC

Upon a round electron sight and sound
Can move along the skies and settle well
Where we'll see nothing go, and there abound
In wires that store our song soft fires that tell
Their hidden spark deep in the dark of night
That gazes at amazing rays so poised
'Tween Now and Having Been, for there is might
Upon a molecule of silence noised.
O flame that hit the lonely night of man
With sense of nothing sensate, with no prong
Of matter made, but weighed with heat that can
The want of all quench in a gentle song,
Move onward in the dark, and mark the hour
That came to be, and saw with singèd pow'r.

Preparing volumes
(for sale in the newly made stall)*

O Master, at the last when we have gone
Our lonely way into the longest home
Of all the waiting earth, when all is done,
And we no more may go but only come
To this Thy one last beck, and when no more
We may o'er moments wield the softest sway
Of seconds bid to settle where before
They travelled o'er the page that turned a day,
Will some tomorrow linger yet awhile
Upon the chargèd current of a line
That bore a hurt and sorrow; will a smile
Beam yet where once 'twas shed, when beams
could shine,
Or will the morrow ne'er a sorrow know
And bid these tomes to yawning æons go?

*And meditating on I Kings 2:2.

131

Adéline*
(«Je veux rester avec toi!»)

Ô petit rien, rayon de ton Dieu
Et trace de ce Maître de nos jours
Qui s'arrêta un moment en ce lieu
Béni par toi, consacré pour toujours
Par ce divin sourire que tu fus,
Un jour, un instant fait de souvenirs
Qui sauront revenir, car il a plu
A l'Éternel de me laisser tenir
Un ange une heure échappé de ce cour
Qui nous attend un jour, car je L'ai vu,
Visage de Sa Face, et cet amour
De quoi tu étais fait me devint plus
Qu'un frottement, qu'un froissement qui passe,
Car même un rien parfois trop embrasse.

*Nièce du frère Dominique, légèrement handicapée

132

Venite seorsum

O! for a taste of distant yesterday,
When sound was still and bounded was the all
By walls wherein no call e'er found a way
Through wire and button round and pressure small
To press upon the whole that soul can touch
And travel to the ravelled nerves of man
That would with but a thought but linger such
As length of thought at rest knows best it can. ..*
O! word of gentle whisp'ring, heard to be
The stilling of much noise, here poised is sound
Again upon the volumes that I see
In tranquil corners of much learning bound—
O bliss! I shall return to this soft land
Where all the years in ink distilled still stand.

*At this point Fr Prior came in and uttered
this unexpected sentence: "Je pense que ce serait
bien que vous fassiez le doctorat tout de suite après
l'Ordination".

Learning to sing Mass

Upon a star there are the long gone years
Of light, of might of fission, that come still
Across the tranquil dark, for here appears
On this night's retina the first night's Will.
O Ancient of all days, I see Thy hand
On this the steady mark that is to come
Upon my soul anon, and on this land
Of sorrow deep I peep yet t'ward my home.
For though I shall Thee hold and shall Thee call
From 'yond these yonder spheres, I here am not
For ever to be held, and droplets small
Of Godhead that made all are all the lot
Of one that in the universe is held
'Tween what is grasped and what is not beheld.

O bliss! O bliss! O utterness of bliss!
That this shall be and never cease to be,
And that a morrow that one day did miss
Should come again and e'er remain to see
Each dawn yet to be born well consecrate
The Master of the æons where He comes
Into these little hands—Aha! to wait
Upon a word wherein the cosmos roams—
This is to hold the ropes of all the earth
And toy with joy of rayons that come well
To this old vale of tears where veiled is mirth
By screens that I shall touch there where this bell
Rings yet our fathers' song: this long, long home

Is all I have.
          I have it.
                  It will come.

A word that changed a life*

The Lord of all the earth stands on the globe
He fashioned on an æon long ago,
And though the sons of Adam darkly probe
The mists of mystic light, and dimly know
The Maker of all time, there come yet some
Stray sparkles of a darkliness too old
To be forgotten quite, and there yet come
Strange glisters small where all at night is told.
O Light! O Light! O Might that holds the world
And finds a way to shine when all is still,
Ignite the shaft of but a wafted word
And change the all within the range of will
That chinked and opened bathes thus in the tide,
The flood, the Blood, that from a dead God sighed.

*Andrea, retreatant, had been away from the
sacraments many years.The Lord gave a
miraculous sign during the night after the return,
itself the consequence of a word.

Letter from home

Within a syllable there lies a sound
Well known, when owned were once the acres green
In which we grew and grew, in which we found
The magic of a life, and what was seen
By eye and ear and nostril opened wide
Upon the shapes of home is seen again
By cells where dwells the all that shall abide
For ever ever more in one lone brain.
O! language that speaks twice, and sings anon
Upon the unwrapped page, O! script oft read
And known well to contain what rocked a son
Long, long ago ere words were ever said,
Will e'er an hour return where this soft light
Shall warm no more an aelwyd once so bright?

27/8, St Monica.
(An *aelwyd* is a hearth.)

Y cofio
(29/8/72)

Daw dydd y daeth dy ddyddiau oll i fod
Dan briod we, dan gysgod nef a roed
Am hyn o oes i ddau; daw awr y nod
A roddwyd ar y ddalen, awr yr oed
Lle unwyd llwybrau oes, awr fer a roes
Sêl nefoedd hen, a gwên y Crëwr maith
Ar rymusterau cudd, ac er nad oes
Ond dau o'r tri a fu yn rhan o'r daith,
Y mae i'r oedfa hon rhwng doe a doe
Yfory sydd i ddod, ryw ryfedd hedd,
Cans er nad yw ein hynaf yn ein hoe,
Ond yn ei dawel hun, ei dawel fedd,
Y mae i chwarter canrif awr a fydd
Yn dyner ar y dagrau wlychai'n dydd.

Verba volant
(Ellen's call)

O voice well known that callest from afar,
To know when it shall be, when thou shalt see
The moment of all time, here where there are
Not many accents known, I twice hear thee,
For though thou comest to see all things die,
There is a gentle sparkle in a sound
That for a distant presence yet does sigh
But for a morrow gone to be refound.
O eyes all pure, so sure where He would lead,
What dint of hinting Providence did bring
Your gazing from afar at this my need
For but a heart that gleaned a little thing?
We are alone upon a lonely world,
But friend and friend can send much on a word.

The dove on the window-sill

(after preaching)

O little creature, chatter for thy King
And teach me what to do without a word.
Coo on and on and in thy cooing bring
A thought for what is held in what is heard.
Great Dewi heard thee come and saw thee go
As free as this thy wing, and it is told
That he upon a growing mount did know
The pow'r of some invention very old.
For megaphone came not and was not made
To capture man's strayed sound, but found was here
A strange contriving where huge striving played
With pulsèd wisdom wherein Wings were near.
For in a world where simple were the days
The earth would stretch to catch a word that strays.

The old confessional

How many sins have crossed this little grille
That stands aloft alone 'tween Heav'n and Hell?
How oft was Blood that on this cross lies still
Shed on a gaping chasm ere a knell
O'er blasted æons rang? How oft did He
Through these weak pores soft pass and cancel all
That could the demons sate in damnèd glee
At what was not revoked in moments small?
Great elegance is not in this wee box
That holds the skies at large, yet charged is this,
Each splinter and each crack, and all Hell rocks
With irritation strong at swindled bliss
That had no right to be, that should not be,
For such dry rot dries not Eternity.

The slip of paper
(with the news about Lady Diana)

A while has passed since last I smiled on thee
In verse and charmèd rhyme, and time has gone
Into the dark that caught thee: History
Within a night was writ, and naught was done
Of this bright Future that then lay ahead
When sweet nineteen thee struck, for plucked was all
At speed of blazèd wrecking: this blest head
Then kissed and well caressed this night did maul.
We sing an hour the song of woman kind
When man is kind as yet and when the dawn
Unborn yet lies afresh, and flesh need find
No reason but its own dim Age to scorn,
But Age must come, and lie upon the page
Of archives inked a night of whitest rage.

Virginity

A joy is made of little particles,
And what needs not too much with such is filled.
The curse and bliss of man's own molecules
Of need to deep need sent, when left well stilled,
Unused upon this land, and never felt
By heart and mind 'hind other gazing plunged,
Leave virgin regions free, and what need melt
In ne'er a human touch at whiles is lunged
On Thee, my veilèd Love, there where Thou art
In all Thine essence dense on this Thy throne
Of particles disguised, for though there part
From this the heart that no known heart did own
Betimes a sigh unheard, a sigh unmade,
I sigh shall ne'er that e'er I with This played.

Quiet

A life were but a simple game to play
Today, were it well studied and well known.
A life is all of nothing blown away
Into a myriad parts, not one its own.
A life is doubly used, and ill abused
Are moments in their coming where they go
Into their frittered firing, ever fused
In their once chargèd pow'r an hour to glow.
A life is many moments never held
For that we held too many when they came,
And life was never known, for ne'er beheld
Was this one ancient truth that stands the same
Upon the tomb of living that we were,
For living was best lived where less did stir.

**Quis mihi det ut exarentur in libro
stylo ferreo, vel celte sculpantur in silice?**

(Job 19:23–24, Office of the Dead)

When I look back upon the shapes of yore
Here chiselled on the page, where age grows old
With but a moment's growing; when before
My eyes the sighs of Yesterday are told
In molecules that inked them where they cried
A day or two long gone; when song is heard
Again within the little lines where ride
The tremors of a joy hushed in a word,
And when I think what could have been perhaps
In cell and hell of penance, where no sound
But Heav'n itself did listen, then there taps
With this old chime that cometh in its round
A something made of hurt, yet hurt we must,
And hurt can last a little in our dust.

Fidelity
(Ellen's wait at Dublin airport in mid-winter)

A day there was and is—for in the mind
It has not died away—when time stood still,
Not for an instant lingering behind
The moment of its coming, but until
An hour into an hour sev'n times had grown,
Sev'n yawnèd times, yet chimes turned not away
Two feet from their long standing all alone
Upon a word that trust would not betray.
"I will" is all the morrow of the will
Of one whose utt'rance stands, and, little one,
In this unmeasured standing, standing still
While nothing, no-one, came, while sound was none
Save one that sounded still, I have beheld
A long awaiting, waiting to be held.

Ἑύρηκα

I have a secret found that sound held not
In its oft loudest coming; I have heard
A message that no eager page could plot
Upon the gazing brain by markings stirred.
I have, my Friend, the end of all things found
In this the sacred myst'ry that here shone
Upon my calmèd mind, for every sound
Was into gazing turned, where 'twas outshone.
I heard, my God, as here I listened well
To naught but hearing's sound, that all is here,
Here, even here, the all that all doth tell,
And that the door to allthing is full near.
For 'tis the art of being, being all
A nothing made of nothing hugely small.

And that the door to allthing... Cf Julian of Norwich

Midnight

To know that in the dark a little light
Will softly burn, that oft a virgin yearn
Unuttered and unknown, at deep of night
Shall peep upon the regions man shall learn
Ne'er once to tread, ne'er once to feel or know,
And that a garden sealed will calmly lie
Untravelled and untaught its fruit to show
To aught beneath a thoughtless moonlit sky—
To know that in a life, life did pass o'er
A little land unclaimed, and that no mind
Kept vigil in the dark, that not a roar
Of need did feed on this bliss left behind,
It is, my friend, to know thee to the end,
For I have known what thou didst never send.

Closer
(Tridentine initiation)

Not once, not twice, were gestures such as these
About a Godhead made, nor fades the day,
The distant dawn on dawn that Hist'ry sees
In these rites rise again, where hid wings play
With essences untold that we make bold
To call into a corner of the globe
By movements well rehearsed, by sounds that hold
In all their whispered strength the High King's robe...
O! cov'ring of a kingdom yet to come,
And yet come now at last where waiting was
Long, very long, in longing that for some
Seemed long past hope, this groping this morn has
The heavy signs of blessing old restirred,
And I the muttered cent'ries overheard.

The eighth again
(of September)

This day has come before, and it has been
A place of many meetings, for it saw
The moments rent asunder when was seen
Too much for but a brittle part of yore.
O hinge of heavy æons! We are not
All present in a day, when cast away
Are days that hang on this, when bliss forgot
Is hell of double hurting left for aye.
O! blunder that shall thunder evermore
O'er gath'ring clouds of sorrow, morrows long
Shall gaze on this thy face, that, glancing o'er
A choice of loaded weight, spared ne'er a song
For what a noise of years would e'er lament,
For what a poisèd second ever rent.

We have been here before, and time has struck
The hours into this shape that they must bear
Tomorrow and tomorrow, for strange luck
Or dint of high Permission nodding there
Behind the hills of Hist'ry, cast a look
Of patient heavy groaning where we walk
On maps of hapless moves, as on this book
Of life unwrit we e'er the story balk.
And yet, O Finger of the script long writ,
Is there a spark of wisdom where the mad
Are given leave to strut, and this high fit
Of highest madness made to make us sad
For evermore, is it for ever known
As best, for that its Author knew His own?

Postulant
(from El Salvador)

Come, trav'ller, come and stay with us a while,
A little while that is eternity,
For that we thither go, and this fond smile
That brother gives to brother comes to thee
From 'yond the skies that wait where some have gone,
Gone on and on and on to where we go
On this old path well trod, for oft was done
The day that thou henceforth shalt ever know.
O! grace wherein a Face here shone again
On one that moved afar o'er land and sea:
There is perhaps a molecule of pain
In these tears that I saw, yet come with me
Into this distant past that lies ahead,
And safe on this soft æon rest thy head.

Unclaimed

(Ellen's silent nursing of baby Giovanni)

I did behold a hold that held the world
One time when mimed was all that could be said,
When home was far from home and not a word
Had sense, of aught e'er uttered or aught read.
'Twas when an angel held an angel load,
The one petite, the other very small,
And when a look the smile of Godhead showed
From depth of loving that for love did call.
For I beheld a mother never made
To mother what was there and never came
Into the light of day; I saw a maid
Of virgin white stand softly all the same
Upon another's burden, that an hour
Had laid upon a breast of unblest pow'r.

Poor Clare
(Michela's letter from Siena, on entering)

I see a heart apart from all mankind
Upon the page, and caged for evermore
Is this the soul that wrote a sound too kind
To be too soon forgot. A little door
Has clapped upon the roaming of a will
That in a last fond clasp not deadened quite
Held on to what a kiss left ever still,
Unused and tranquil in thine unreached night.
O! little bond of being, left between
A cloister and a cloister very near
And very far away—a virgin clean
And pure of all man's sharing, in a tear
I saw not, but discerned, did leave a mark,
And wimpled now's the night, and 'twill be dark.

Messe sur le monde
*(face à l'Orient)**

A time and half a time, a little time
Holds me from Thee, my King, and we shall stand
Alone upon the all, for small steps climb
To Greatness where fond cherubs fear to land:
This is the stone where oft this miracle
Was heard times past to pass; this is the home
Away from Home where but a particle
Shines in the heart wherein strange myriads come.
I have come home, my God, and yesterday
Stands safely at the door, for evermore
I shall at dawn Thee touch, as touch did they
That knew how this to handle long before.
For long is not our song, and we hand on
A little secret that o'er old dawns shone.

*Cf Job 1:11

After Midnight Office

Within the night the might of man awake
Beholds a land unseen, and all that moves
Beneath the sleeping sky a sigh doth make
Heard by the stars alone, for distant loves
Move closer in the dark, and we are not
As still at dead of night as in the day
When movements great bid wait what is forgot
By eyes by trinkets filled as trinkets may.
I hear afar a heart that never was
Poised well for a caress, for none did bless
Its beat unheard with such a word as has
A pow'r of double beating: but a tress
Or two of greying hair unfondled there
I know shall lie this night, awaiting e'er.

Tu es sacerdos . . . in æternum
(Printing invitation)

O! Mystery that History doth make
With these sealed moves syllabic that we draw
Upon the page that sees us one road take
For e'er and not another—but a flaw
A word unsaid or muttered when best hid,
The chain of heavy seconds shatters aye,
And age did oft rage long where youth's song bid
A destiny go ever on its way.
Yet I shall not regret this little hour
That weds my soul to Godhead for all time,
And I behold already some great pow'r
Made all of loving deep that bids me climb
And stand alone upon a land of light
That waits, my sister, 'yond our ageing night.

Faculties?
(for forgiveness)

A vibrant cord, a column made to sing,
Can many echoes move where depths are heard
High in these rafters high, and words can bring
Upon a pulpit small a call where stirred
A corner of a soul, a region swept
Not often and not well: a hell foretold
Can tingle yet awhile where demons slept
In peace where sin did cease e'en to be bold.
And now, milord, again a little sound,
Should it in time be made, could chimèd years
And æons long, that could for aye redound
Unto the praise of folly, in hell's ears
Redeem in but a beam of gentle sound
Wherein a heavy heart a healing found.

Tudalen

Y mae i ddalen fud ryw uchel floedd
I'r galon gloff, lle hoff yw tawel sain
Ac atsain synau lawer unwaith oedd
Yn teithio'r rhod, ac er ond bod yn fain
Wna'r tenau las fodolaeth sydd yn don
Ar donfedd gudd y fron, daw papur gwyn
Â mwy na phlŷg neu ddau, cans etyb hon—
Nid â mwyn ffurf ac ysgrif, ond â'r oll
A drig mewn cell a chlasdy, lle nad oes
Ond llais yr echdoe pell sydd heddiw 'ngholl
Yn cyffwrdd mur a mur â chur y Groes.
Mi wn, fy Nuw, mi wn mai hyn a fydd;
Mi wn am sain rhyw ddeigryn ffyddlon cudd.

Clementina
(et la double grille du Carmel)

O! joie de la souffrance, enfance d'ange
Qui pars demain pour ce grand continent
D'obscurité voilée, où ces phalanges
De séraphins couronnés maintenant
T'attendent, petit rien, là où sont
Les ailes éthérées qui sur les âges
À venir, à revenir, voileront
La Face qui t'attire en ces parages.
O! grille qui t'enlève à mon regard
De frère, qui t'a connue, qui t'a vue,
T'a vue à fond, où fondait tout ce nard
D'amour, de larmes fait: aura-t-il plu
Au Maître de ce jeu de prendre en toi
Ce qu'autrefois sa joie eût fait de moi?

Garde le silence, et le silence te gadera*
(Visage sculpté à Paray-le-Monial)

Ô petit mot qui dis le tout de tout
Sans rien dire—et qui le dis depuis
Le jour de ta naissance, où l'un de nous
A su en toi plaider sans moindre bruit:
Ta voix bâillonnée, là où vit le temps
À jamais ciselé en vraie sourdine,
Me parle et me reparle sur un ton
Trop fort pour mes oreilles, pourtant fines—
Car sur les ondes des grands souvenirs
Laissés ici, tracés ici en toi,
J'entends un bruit de siècles à venir
Sans bruit tout comme toi, tout comme moi
Hier, hier, avant-hier, quand Dieu
M'eût scellé pour tout demain en ce lieu.

*Paroles familières, riches de souvenirs de ce *lieu*,
la Grande Trappe.

It will be
. . . soon

Upon an æon long I'll take my rest
And think again on what might once have been,
And o'er the dim horizon of the West
Of sunsets ever gone I shall between
The days there ever lived the others see
That never came to be, that never had
A name upon the map Eternity
Plots slowly on the course that moments bad.
And I shall hear again a day like this
Full softly in my ears that sleep in peace
Say, "'Twas a touch, a pull, a little bliss
That mattered in the end," for matters cease
To matter much beside a God agaze,
For I'll catch in a touch a Christ ablaze.

Dona, Padre onnipotente . . .
(consecratory words)

What is a day upon the universe
When Time has been so long? What is an hour
That comes and goes for better or for worse
And wields but o'er a spot a little pow'r?
What is a moment when so many more
Have come on Chronos' tide and gone away
To where they'll ever be, as were of yore
The minutes waiting long to have their say?
What is a touch when many such have been
On parts not often touched, on parts not known
To be so wide awake, when all was seen
That need be known on earth by two alone?
Yet 'tis an hour like any on a day
That in a second split sears Time for aye.

Still

When we are still the world goes on its way
Unheard, nay doubly heard, for it need not
At all times have our help, and sometimes may
Move onward on its course when we're forgot.
When we are still the world is very wide,
And there is room to hide beside the blast
That can be heard afar, when we but bide
A moment at a time ere time be past.
And when, my God, I wait awhile and let
The all yet happen well without my aid,
And learn e'en in my list'ning to be set
On hearing well the colour of each shade,
Then I perceive a meaning sensed and known,
For I receive alone when all alone.

Alone

I cannot be alone as I would be
For e'er – it ne'er could be – , yet 'tis not far
The solitude of soul, the whole of me
That need not be elsewhere, for some there are
That entered this vast land with ne'er a cell
Or wall to call them home to where we walk
Unheeded and unknown, and I see well
That Hiddenness is but the way we talk.
For Master, I have heard in this Thy breath
Upon mine inward ear, that very near
Is this mine ancient dream: 'tis but a death,
A dying of all sound, a lying here
Where none may enter in, where none may come,
For one alone of Silence builds a home.

Last Sunday as deacon
(at our High Mass)

O peace! I have found all! I have come home,
And 'twas not very far – 'twas at the door
Of this the tent of meeting where there come
Again at whiles the wings I heard before
Hard by the Master watching: I have been
Alone with these my brethren oft a time
When youth was strong and truth in fire was seen,
Yet 'twas ere now ne'er giv'n hereto to climb.
For on the morrow stands the Lord of all
Awaiting with the hand that made the years,
And here anon a syllable too small
To hold the cosmos well will touch my ears,
– My ears, I say, my hands, my singèd soul –
And utter naught will Godhead caught control.

Y cwmwl

Yfory ac yfory eto ddaw,
Ond ni fydd oriau bellach fel y ddoe,
Cans dydd ni ddaw heb i mi yn fy llaw
Ddal Duwdod mewn eiliedyn sydd yn cloi
Galluoedd gwyrth a gras dan lais a nod
A drefnwyd gan hir gof: na, dof yn ôl
At wawr canrifoedd pell, a gwell yw bod
Am awr yn nefol ffôl, os hyn sydd ffôl.
Cans yma yn y cwmwl clywaf rai
A roddodd gynt eu traed ar farmor maen
Ein hallor hen, a gwên megis pe bai
O bellter yr eonau fu o'r blaen,
Ac eto sydd, ac eto fydd fan hyn
Yn sefyll fel y ddoe dan Friwsion gwyn.

(Monte Oliveto)

Watching and waiting
(in retreat, Monte Oliveto)

I hear upon the night the centuries
That passed this way pass on, but not pass by.
I hear in this old eve the melodies,
That touched oft, oft an ear, move 'neath the sky.
I hear, my God where flickers and where burns
This ancient light, the might that made my soul,
And in this night that softly dawnward turns
I hear what I would hear: I hear the whole.
For though, hid Love of all, the voice is small
That Godhead makes in passing, pass it will
Into my chrismèd hands at this high call
Of pontifex and custom, for 'tis still
The small, small voice of Horeb that comes nigh,
And for this eve long hours did long, long sigh.

Φώς 'ιλαρόν

O! light, O! blessed Trinity,
O! might, O! primal Unity,
Our softer fire now goes its way,
Receive our hymn at close of day.

To Thee we sang at rise of dawn,
In Thee its rays we praised at morn:
A prostrate glory now receive
Ere this eve's rays for e'er we leave.

O! Majesty, O! Trinity,
O! light of all Eternity,
This eventide we lift Thy praise
Upon the rays of ancient days.

(Melody; *O lux beata*)

Simplify

I have a secret heard within this place
Beside this little lamp that wards my King.
I have gazed long at this the well-hid Face,
And sometimes in the dark I would Thee sing:
For Thou art near, my God, and nearer still
As hours Thy mighty hand move t'ward my head,
And in a calmèd corner much can fill
The empty ear that hears what is not said.
'Tis this, my silent Lord, that Thou didst say
Deep, deep where all is known: 'twas this Thy word
That, coming, drove full oft a word its way
Into the long unsaid – I heard, I heard
But one small shade of meaning in the dark:
"Enough! Enough!" Enough 'tis hence to hark.

Sufficit

There are not many things I need to know,
But one I need know well; there is not space
'Tween end and hurried end of hours below
These hours twice o'er to wield, nor is there place
To walk two roads at once or twice to come
Upon a moment's journey: we are not
The masters of our morrow, but our home
Is where worn moments lie and are forgot.
Upon this tomb of seconds I behold
Two ways that lie ahead, for when 'tis said,
This sentence that we cry, then is too old
The breath that went astray, for 'twas not led
By sage economy of energy
That wasted not, that hasted not to be.

(In retreat, after visiting graves)

Safe

The everlasting arms nurse æons all
With patience and with care, and all is well
When viewed from very far, for turnings small
Are straight unto the Eyes that journeys tell.
All shall be well, and allthing, every thing
Was cared fot yesterday when we were not
A worry in the world, and we but bring
A little ruffle to an hour forgot.
But there are hours that matter o'er the world,
And this is one, my King, for but a day
Holds matter from a magic of a word
That uttered was ere Time began to say,
"There will be one upon a distant sky
That on a day 'neath these old rays shall lie..."

A book

To read is to be with a buried word
That could have lain unheard – to be alone
And not alone where memories are stirred
On this the page that stores them as its own:
'Tis to be all at listen, all an ear
Of inward hearing well, to answer not
But to be taught beneath a bygone year
By one whose mast'ry did not with him rot.
To write is to speak well without a voice
Across the years that threaten, 'tis to be
A little careful in a little choice
Of shapes that hold a sound that some may see
Tomorrow and tomorrow where we are
Not seen again, but heard afar, afar.

Ubi venit plenitudo temporis
(Adoring and rehearsing)

'Tis th'eve of th'eve of all, and in the Blood
That washed the world I stand afresh and wait
At th'altar of the Lamb, for very God
Of very God awaits 'hind heaven's gate.
The thunder of the Word once heard of yore
By prophet and by sage, by priest and king,
Awaits, awaits 'hind this yet sealèd door
O'er which my angel friend soft spreads his wing:
Tomorrow, this Thy hand, Thy voice, Thine all
O small and hid Jehovah, shall me reach
From o'er the eras gone, and one vast call
Heard well by waiting cherubs shall hence teach
The molecules of time to move along
A path here traced by but a bar of song.

(Monte Oliveto, in retreat)

After the moment
(...and immediately after first Absolution)

O King of kings, O Lord of all that is,
Is this all true? Is this all happening?
A word, a touch, a paragraph of his,
Did it so loudly through the æons ring?
It did, my Lord, and I did feel Thy hold
Upon my aching soul, for in a spark
I saw, I saw with sight of light untold
My being torn to Heav'n for one deep mark.
I did, O Alpha, for a second see
As 'twere the face of ancient Godhead there
Where I was briefly caught, and I saw Thee
The Ancient of all days enthronèd there
Unchanged, unhurried, waiting for this word
That every soul through kingdom come well
heard.

The first time

O light! O might! O whiteness of my God
Here coming, coming, come upon a word!
O! clasping of my Lord here where have trod
The feet of sacred armies now unheard,
Yet heard again in these soft fiery sounds
That worked here in my hands an ancient change
That angels find e'er new, for there surrounds
This nought of nought here bent a denseness strange:
My God, as I o'er particles here gazed,
They did here cease to be, and I beheld
With ne'er a ray of sight what all amazed
My friend here at my side, for he ne'er held
The Godhead as his ward, nor did the sword
Of angel speech e'er reach this Wound outpoured.

(All Saints)

Due da confessare

(All Souls)

O! Blood, in but a word that washes all
In this old flood of cleansing, where the scars
And stains of sons of men, of great and small,
Were hid for e'er, though bared 'neath gazing stars:
O! stream where cleansed in time were all that went
Along this heavy way where we now prayed
'Side stones of heavy sleep, where heaved and rent
In heaviness full grown, were hours here weighed...
Great God, the nod of æons at a sound
Made by a larynx weak, that these seek here
In this last christic breath, hath all hell bound,
And in a syllable two gates are near.
For onward can a trav'ler go again
From sentence brief to Sentence of all pain.

High Mass towards the Orient

There is a peace upon the earth at last,
And skies have time to be. There is no haste
Or matter great to work, for we have cast
Our anchor in the deep, and we have faced
The Godhead in full force: we have held high
The Lamb upon His throne, – nay, we did own
The voice that He had not, and did bend nigh
O'er particles that some were better shown.
For 'twas a miracle that moved my feet
In distant days 'vangelic to this place
Of mighty Roman air, and I now meet
In inches 'fore my face a hallowed space
Where gaze did gaze at gaze upon this land
Where man alone with th'All Alone did stand.

The hands
(across the grille)

Poor lonely Clare that held what held thy Lord
By all within thy reach, reached by no man
Save Him that will thee wed, whose chrismic word
With unction strong through these here slowly ran -
Near, angel, here – thou couldst not let these go
As quickly as they came to thy dark world
Of fondling none, yet of a touch we know,
For we far from this earth have now been hurled.
Siena, this thy ground is hallowed well,
And I shall this my life on thy stones lay,
For though far, far from home, I now can tell
The shape of this trod morrow of our day.
For yesterday was made of souls like these,
And there's a touching that can angels please.

Near...here: the Cathedral.

177

First time alone
(in an old little church near Orvieto, shrine of the miracle)

O Master, here at last I stand alone
With but an angel guard, and I Thee call
Without another voice: this silent stone
Laid by another age, this heavy wall
Built on the faith of centuries gone by,
Thought not that they this miracle would hold
That we today in freshness bid here lie
In but a sound or two of magic old.
O! Chalice of much love, where many came
'Neath Calvary to catch the Blood of God
In silence as it fell, the same, the same
From hand to priested hand, here where have trod
The feet of many that have long gone on:
The change I saw not well, yet knew, 'twas done.

Latin Mass

(served by Dom Alban at Prinknash)

Back, back again to minutes that stood still
Upon this little corner of the world
In distant days when freshness pulled the will
To acts of folly, wherein all was hurled
Into a forcèd rest, a forcèd feed,
A forcèd, forcèd wait, wherein came not
The cloister wanted well – O! little seed
Grown in another land, 'twas ne'er forgot:
The first of every love ne'er lost its flame,
And had a word been said, this would have been
The home of stable years, yet 'twas the name
That thou, my father, uttered that came 'tween
What should perhaps have been and what did be
The ever having been of History.

Name: Carthusians

The old familiar parish
(St Mary of the Angels)

This is the altar whereon many dreams
Did linger o'er long hours: 'twas here that love
Was strong, when yet the morrow's coming beams
Did dawn on waiting dawn, for here did move
The might that moved the world, and I recall
That oft as morn soft shone and eve did die
I'd hide and huddle well and here Thee call,
Good Master, 'hind this veil where Thou didst lie.
Yet I thought not that I one day would come
Again to mem'ry's land, or here would stand
To call Thee gently back to this our home
Made all of things well known, or that this hand
Would hold the Chalice that my father held
Here, even here, where years and old tears welled

(Cardiff, before Mass)

The Chalice, the Tabernacle, the old pew
(the same, after Mass)

O! odour, O! fond wood, O! place of prayer
Wherein so much was known – O! Paradise
Of that first burning flame, sweet haven fair
Where all was safe beneath the smiling skies –
Is this all true? Is this old dream still here
Awaiting my return? To hold and hold
The Cup that I knew well, to be so near
To yesterday and to a thought so old –
This is to be much moved where all is still
In stillness that said all, and waited well
Till it should be as bid an ancient Will
That this meandered morrow all could tell:
For, Lord of love, I have here loved, much loved,
And talk comes not too well when too much moved.

Uchel Allor Dolgellau
(lle y clywyd yr alwad, haf 1991)

Ragluniaeth hynod hen a hir dy law
Ar holl droadau'r rhod, mi wn dy fod
Yn gweld o bell, yn gweld yn well a ddaw
Yn rhan o'r patrwm hwn, a bod dy nod
Ar ffurf pob un yfory fu ynghlwm
Wrth arfaeth faith y Drefn osodwyd ddoe
Ym mherfedd yr eonau ddeil yn drwm
Eu pwysau ar yr oriau sydd yn troi...
O Babell hen gyfarfod! – dyma'r fan
Y bu i'r 'fory hwn gael ffurf a llun:
Dy sibrwd glywais gynt, ac, er yn wan,
Yn ddim ger grym Awdurdod a nerth Dyn,
Gwn adlais rhyw hen lais lefarai, "Bydd,
Fe fydd, cans ond y Fi a ddeil y dydd."

Solemn Mass

(at Dolgellau Carmel)

O virgin light! O sight of virgin prayer
Where angels softly tread, where breath aflame
Spreads all on being nought, and when the fair
Is fair for One alone, and where a name
Means all to not a man – this is the place
Where grace did pull two hearts and where the all
Was fought by breasts unknown, and where a Face
Unseen did doubly beam in twice a call.
O Carmel! – this is home for oft a bride,
And though Prémontré's incense calls me home,
I could yet linger and 'fore this Tent hide
A tear too deep to shed, for one did roam
From this thy safest hearth to darkest earth,
To mingle with a magic of strange mirth.

Gellilydan

Y mae i fan a lle fwy nag a wêl
Y llygad noeth; y mae i liw a llun
A welwyd droeon gynt, pan glywyd sêl
Y fendith oddi fry, ryw hud a lŷn.
Ac y mae mewn hen wedd ryw hedd a gwên
A ddaw â Ddoe yn ôl: y mae fan hyn,
Yn rhandir pethau hoff, goffáu sydd hen
A phurdeb eto ddeil, fwyn angel gwyn.
Cans aros wnaethost di, a rhoddi'r oll
I weld yr orig hon, ac yn dy law
Fe ddeliaist hyn o gariad aeth yngholl,
Nid yma'n ddyn, ond yma'n win a ddaw
Yng ngair hen ffrind y ddoe yn Waed dy Dduw,
Ac yn ein dagrau, Ef oedd wrth y llyw.

Roscrea

O! odour of fond yesterdays long gone,
And ne'er to come again, O! memory
In air and matter held, O! work undone
In workings of an hour, O! History
Unwrit and ever hit from th'orbit plain
That o'er this blessèd cloister turned and turns
And will turn gently on again, again
Without one soul that late its error learns...
'Tis well to hold my Lord upon this world
Within the world of morrows that roll on
Without our aid, yet much was hence once hurled
Into the long unknown, there where had shone
A smile held but a little while, a day,
A little day that took my days away.

Kindness, such kindness

A friend is put a part that went away
And still remained, and travelled o'er the waves
Of time and distance long, a buried day
That ne'er did fully die: a hand that waves
Sends moments on their way for evermore,
And though a tear be little in the sea,
There gathers in a drop a heavy store
Of sorrow that must ever, ever be.
Fly onward, angel, to thy greenest land
Of morrows that will dawn without my aid,
But know that this fond smile will ever stand
Upon the screen that solitude well made.
For though I travel home to this my God,
There are some parts of earth that He hath trod.

(On the boat, bearing the new Chalice)

Diolch

(Moving out of Bangor station)

Farewell, fair land; fade, fade into the past
And come not back to haunt and taunt the mind
Of Solitude, for there are scenes that last
Long after they have been, for left behind
Was ne'er a day that was, and this old face
That held the whole world safe, shines softly on
As long as it may yet, for though the space
'Twixt Time and Time to come be not yet gone,
There cannot be long hours ahead of us,
Kind mother of my days, and hours have ways
Of moving otherwise, for moments thus
Come sometimes nevermore, and silent days
And years and mem'ries long at times hang on
To but a little fading smile that shone.

Vatican
(Lateran Vicariate)

A word of highest pow'r can turn the world
Into an orbit new, and there shall be
Tomorrow many morrows hither hurled
That yesterday thought little e'er to see.
A word, I say, both written and soft blown
Across the wires of sound, hath found a home
Within a list'ning ear too long alone,
And ear to brain to mouth hath whispered, "Come."
So be it, Lord, hid ever at the wheel
Of Fortune vast, for cast is now the die,
And this old Tiber let us cross, to steal
A one last vict'ry, for which years did sigh.
For youth long waited to be doctored here,
And yesterday is very, very near.

O Bonitas!

(Santa Maria degli Angeli)

A vow was made within this precinct strange
That holds old goodness still, but 'twill not be
As quickly as it came, for 'neath the range
Of happ'nings to be grasped I do not see
The path of solitude so clearly shown
As 'twas when I came by, for Will and will
Were wed since then upon a sacred stone,
And I may not now will e'en to be still.
Yet there is p'haps a hope in this small spark
Of light and love meridian that came here
In fond Hiberian tint, for but a mark
Can hold at whiles an old smile very near,
And should this cell yet open I would go
For ever and for aye the way I know.

> *Hiberian*: Spanish tint, that of my former Master,
> now Prior of another Charterhouse.

Romeward bound

(on the train)

It is a while since last I walked this way
Into a land of letters, and to this
The City of all time, where ancient day
Did dawn upon fond youth with dreams of bliss
That now again take flesh, in freshness such
As newly chrismèd hands alone may know,
For though for this late hour days waited much,
There is a faint delight in eve's last glow:
For o'er a year or two the silent page
At morn, at noon, at night shall be my friend,
And company shall be the buried sage
That calmly shall speak on unto the end
Of this beginning made four winters past,
Four winters and four summers oddly vast.

The Vatican's majestic walls

*(Congregation for Religious,
early morning)*

The heart of Christendom is seldom still,
And as the world turns over yet a day
Of History begun, the gentle thrill
Of Yesterday is heard here where for aye
The morrow lingers long, for song so old
As this the patient bliss of days gone by
Into a dusk their own—a story told
And told and told again behind the sky—Is new
again this morn, this crack of morn
Whereon breaks yet an era, yet a time
To be a child again, in newness born
Of christic freshness made, for this great chime
Of Petrine weight and sound redounds o'er all
The hurry of a hominide so small.

(Completed during adoration before the Bd
Sacrament in St Peter's, meditating on Mt 6:25–34.)

Alma Mater

This place I have known well, this place I know
And love for what it was and what it knew
When knowledge was new-found, for here we grow
Again where many greener heads once grew . . .
O! thought rethought, old feeling felt again
Upon these well trod steps, these archèd ways
To angles of spent hours, to sweetest pain
Of learning dense condensed in measured days—
I thought not thee to see, Alma, on earth
Again ere I went on to learning's Home,
And though 'tis late, a little little mirth
I shall allow to tingle and to come
Into a breast that rested not too well,
And meddled with a molecule of Hell.

(After returning to Angelicum)

Maestro Adamo, una parola

O voce del silenzio che fu
La vita di un'anima ormai
Sepolta, sconosciuta, e, quaggiù
Svanita, seppellita, spenta, mai
Sentita né udita dove noi
Seguiamo queste righe cariche
D'Ieri, che ci vengono da voi,
Autori di perenni musiche . . .
O voce sminuita, stenta—qui
Sentita, rincarnata, resa, là,
Presenza dell'assente—ente, sì,
Vivente fra di noi nell'Aldilà,
Ti sento, anima, nell'anima
Di qualche riga debolissima.

Facsimile

Technology is knowledge highly sprung,
And where there is much pain again a sound
Made all of sigla sent and calmly hung
Upon a well-hid wave a way here found
To stroke the inward soul, for I can see
Upon a page electric many signs,
And I behold tomorrow's history
Writ 'tween the tender shape of chargèd lines.
Eternal city, Rome, be home again
For yet a year or two; let loneliness
For hard thought set apart be gentle pain
To heal monastic din and heaviness
Made all of many things, where few need be,
For none but the alone was ever free.

(En cellule)

Implement

(a new computer)

A little box of tricks, a mouth to be
Tomorrow heard again, a head to hold
The thought of yesterday, a memory
To stand, withstand all time, and to withhold
The waves of thought from long oblivion's night,
And all the might of knowing to restore
Upon the fragile page that Age from sight
At times from Time keeps well: this here thou'lt store.
For but a day now holds sweet Babylon
And solitude of thinking very high
And deeply on and on and gently on
Upon the Master's voice, and each shed sigh
Gleaned on the silent page thy head shall call
And, small though it may be, well, well recall.

(Eve of departure for Rome)

195

An interview
(at Maryknoll)

To be alone and happy for a while
With parchments of rolled years, to stand aside
And at the hurried æons softly smile
And pause 'tween Now and Then, to hide, to hide
The head from noise beside the Hidden's home
And be all thought again, and be all one—
This, this, all this in this one small word, "Come"
That came this day and in a good face shone . . .
O! Master, I did see where we shall meet
At this Thy Throne, and where I'll hear again
The voice of the entombed in strokes complete
With heavy sense that centuries hath lain
Awaiting one to come again this way,
This old, old way as old as but a day.

Last first Mass
(with the contemplativesof perpetual adoration)

A time has come, a time has gone away
Since last I saw this smile and felt these lips
Upon my cheeks soft press: this blessèd day
The ticking oft of seconds gently tips
Into a dusk gone by where here we were
Around this Sun sweet huddled where no light
But this alone did shine, where nought did stir
But this the heavy tapping of the night.
O! virgin lamps still bright where earth rolls on,
I thought not you to feed and you to sign
And these your lips to feel here where has gone
The unguent of a God, for I did pine
Too much when here before to hope 'twould come,
And 'twas thy prayer, hid angel, brought me home.

(Rome, Via Appia Nuova)

Here, even here

*(Latin Mass in St Philip Neri's private chapel
where he would celebrate for two hours.)*

Is this the place where ecstasy would be
A little off the ground? Is this where stood
On thinnest air one given eyes to see
Beyond the veil that shields this Flesh and Blood?
O Philip, is it true that thou wouldst come
And linger for a lengthy while at this
Strange task ne'er giv'n to angels, but to some,
And only some, that bear this mark of bliss?
O Lamb of God, here slain upon a word,
Teach me to wait a while where some have been
Alone with Thee before, where some have heard,
Where some have heard and seen what was not seen
By common eye: for I have time to stand
A little longer on this strangest land.

Il canto di Gesù Cristo
(for the Solemn Profession of two cloistered nuns)

Tra di noi, dentro di noi,
Il cuore di Gesù.
Il cuore, l'amore, la mente di Gesù.

Gesù Cristo, uguale al Padre,
Nell'eternità di eternità,
Non considerò la gloria, la gloria.

Ma spogliò se stesso, ma svuotò se stesso,
Assumendo la forma dello schiavo,
Apparso come uno di noi, come noi.

Ancora più, umiliò se stesso,
Obbediente fino alla morte,
Alla morte della croce, la croce.

Dio dunque lo esaltò
E gli diede un nome al di là
Di ogni altro nome, ogni nome.

Tutto si pieghi ormai sulla terra
Nel nome, nel nome di Gesù,
E ogni lingua proclami Cristo Signore, il Signore.

(Sacro Cuore: per le monache agostinane di Santa Lucia)

La Vergine della Rivelazione
(Tre Fontane, il 12 aprile 1947)

È dunque vera, questa verità
Che non volevo credere, perché
Non era scritta né sentita, là,
–Almeno alle mie orecchie,—
Nel testo sacro dove solo fu
Udita quella Voce che non ha
Né bocca né parola? Gioventù!
Che paradiso la semplicità!
La Vergine che non veniva mai
Sull'orizzonte del credente, che
Sapeva tutto bene, qui ormai
M'insegna delle strane pratiche.
Non so però se anche l'estasi
Sa ben illuminar i lucidi.

Petertide

(On the roof, dusk)

Will this fair City fade into the past
Of what we are, of what we were ahwile
Upon a day, a day that could not last
But could but linger in a distant smile
Called Yesterday, the day that ever was
And shall be evermore, a spectred frame
Of facts by moments writ—the day that has
The vict'ry o'er the æons it did tame . . . ?
O Yesterday, good-bye, bid bygone eves
Rest there where this last goes, rocked by the chime
Of Peter's heavy dome, for Rome here grieves
But little for a little son of time
That bids farewell to but a heaviness,
For that it held awhile a happiness.

Gestapo

What silent cries yet echo in the air
Where pain was great, where hating was all foul
With newly mastered mirth, for there, e'en there
In that dark nether cell did demons prowl
And chuckle at a broken hominide,
A morsel of a man, than which no fly
Was ever better crushed, for angels sighed
Hard by this little place that rent the sky.
O! souls now free form manifold device
And engine of high hell, how well this noon
Do you this gloom recall, and when the vice
Of hardest pressing skill the cravèd boon
Of Will's unconquered snapping did in turn
By one more turn unveil, what did eyes learn?

(Sitting in front of headquar

The pocket stole
(that witnessed many tears)

O matter of small worth, worth all the earth
And all the stars of heav'n, for that the skies
Bend down upon a sound found to be worth
A voyage for a soul all, all the prize
Of damnèd squadrons deep—O fragile cloth,
All mute and all discreet, what hast thou heard?
What bullets of high hell and darkest wrath
Hast thou well shielded at a whisper heard?
By altar, rock and tree, by night, by day,
By busy road and lands where virgins tread,
What sins walked over thee, and found a way
To Blood that mingled with a soul that bled?
And who, ere life be done, shall come again
And leave upon a tear a heavy pain?

All through the night

'Όμματα 'εισίν αστέρες,
        διά νυκτός,
δόξης 'όντες δή 'οπτήρες,
        διά νυκτός,
'η σκοτία γάρ φώς 'έστιν
'εν 'ώ τό καλόν 'ένεστιν·
τό 'αόρατον πάρεστιν
        διά νυκτός.

Χάριν δέ καί 'έχει 'ούτος
        διά νυκτός,
Ώ 'αστήρ καίπερ τοσούτος·
        διά νυκτός,
'ισχυρός 'εί καί 'αρχαίος,
καί 'ημείς τούτου τού φωτός
'έσμεν 'αυγή 'εις 'αλλήλους
        διά νυκτός.

(Melody: *Ar hyd y nos*)

Loquere, Domine: audit servus tuus

Silentium! Silentium!
Sodalis dormientium
In clausula dulcedinis
Stillantis solitudinis.

Hic solus tecum sum
Cum Solo, qui Silentium,
Illudque solum, inhabitat
Eiusque sonum resonat.

O Quies! fac quiescere
In dulci tuo pectore
Hoc pectus quod in strepitu
Quietem quærit sonitu.

O Absens! reple Vacuum!
Fons silens horum fluctuum
Qui in aëre nunc tinniunt –
Audisne tu qui te audiunt?

(V.7)
O vasta devastata Nox!
Minuta murmurata Vox!
Te roboantem in medio
Æternitatis audio.

Exigua Vox sibilans!
Antiqua Aurora rutilans!
En cæcus manum tuæ do
Dum solus mundi in ora sto.

O gutta ex mari Temporis,
Quæ "Vita" a nobis diceris
Heia! in te mersus, auferor
In Orientem e quo orior.

Æterne Solitarie,
In sæculis invarie
Soliloquens cum æonibus,
Nos soli soli te audimus.

(V.5)

O Tacens! Tacens! Loquere!
Inanitas! te capere
Me doce ac hanc præsentiam,
Palpare, ut noscam Essentiam.

O tenebrose Radie!
Micantem hic quotidie
Te cerno – immo, sentio –
Velatum autem Silentio.

Tacentem tacens sentio,
Hic solus cum Silentio
Beatæ Solitudinis -
Solæ Beatitudinis.

Nam solum in solitu
Umbrante multitudine
Alarum Invisibilium,
Non solus, nam cum Solo, sum

(V.11)

Nam Pax cum pace loquitur
Inane solum implebitur:
Auditur raro in strenuis
Susurrus Auræ tenuis.

Resertus in hac cellula,
Deserta quasi in insula,
Abscondor in Abscondito
Ignotus – nisi Incognito.

Lettre incandescente

(Auditu auris audivi de te,
nunc autem oculus meus videt te.*)

Encore un billet de cet Au-delà
Que trop de monde taxe d'être obscur;
Encore une âme envoyée ici-bas,
Séparée toutefois par ce grand Mur
Qu'elle aurait bien voulu pouvoir rompre
Une heure, un instant—juste assez pour faire
Cet acte qui eût seul pu interrompre
Au bout d'un siècle ou deux la grande affaire . . .
«Arrête!» dit cette ombre à la croyante
Qui priait pour la paix d'un esprit cher—
Et qui, hélas, devint la clairvoyante
Qui dut écrire un billet pour l'enfer.
Oui, Oui! Son âme-sœur a dit ceci:
«Écris . . . pour que nul autre n'entre ici!»

**Job 42:5

Meditating after Vigils

(on: τόν ἄρτον ʽημῶν τόν ʼεπιούσιον δός ʽημίν σήμερε

As waking hours restir from blackened calm
To meet in their arousal what one eve
Had slowly stored away, the gentle balm
Of night oblivion and sweet make-believe
Returns from lands hypnotic our stray minds,
And they behold the shores from which they sailed
On voygages unguided, where none finds
A map or record of the pathways trailed.
And this the gentle tapping of the dawn,
That bids us ope our lids to see it smile
At its wrapped gift of living ne'er yet worn,
Is but the kiss of Passing that one while
Now offers to our rested cheeks, lest we
Too quickly stir this day's eternity.

*Mt 6,11

Out of the blue

(A call from Ireland with a personal message
given through a child)

There are in wires small particles of mind
That with but little shifting bid it move
The all of what we are, and we can find
In e'en a handed message moving love
And linger in a warmth of being known
And wanted upon earth—but words from Heav'n
Till recently came not 'neath this old tone,
Nor were these lines to angel peeps oft giv'n.
To think, high Friend, that thou didst deign to smile
Especially for me, and want to say
A word to mortal man, and think awhile
How best to have it said—this is to play
A game with mystic friends I never knew,
And to be rocked by shocks of glory's hue.

Lectio Divina

(Coming across old letter in the sacred pages)

Rest now, good friend, rest on; the time is gone:
No more shall scribblings travel on a page
From where this hand now lies; yet though 'tis done,
The work that they performed, there is not age
Or growing older in the Father's land
Where son meets son that was a son in turn
To Adam that all bore, and this kind hand
That penned a hurried word doth here return,
Not from the tomb, but from the womb of hours,
The ancient calm where all things have an end,
And though where lies that face, the gentle pow'rs
Of loving come no more, this earth can lend
A particle or two to hold a sound
That I will hear again when home is found.

Si tôt, mon frère?
*(La mort subite d'un jeune moine)**

Mon frère, as-tu vu maintenant ce lieu
Si longtemps rêvé? Sais-tu maintenant
Ce que tu voulais savoir? Tes deux yeux
En s'ouvrant sur ce lointain continent,
Qu'ont-ils pu voir? Ce moment fut-il court—
Ce moment qui séparait tous les tiens
Des nôtres qui demeurent? Oui, tu cours,
Étienne, mais un autre attrappe bien.
Tu es très occupé ce soir à laisser faire
Ce Temps, qui ne fut donné ici-bas
Qu'en petits bouts trop courts pour pouvoir plaire
A cette Hâte, amie de l'Au-delà
Qui voit venir encore un grand coureur
Sautant l'Éternité en sa fureur.

*Nous étions l'un à côté de l'autre à la Trappe.

A new Reverend Father
(at the Grande Chartreuse)

To be again a part of Thee, my God,
All in a corner hid, where none may come,
In but an angle of the world where trod
The feet of angels that have now gone home
To where we all shall come—to be once more
Where Yesterday was bright, where light was all
The force of growing day, to ope the door
To dungeons of deep bliss where myriads call—
Twould be a joy too great for one small breast
That heard too much and saw too much awhile,
For, God in hiding, I can never rest
Until I hide in Thee, and see Thee smile
Again as once did beam what can but be
Known where alone no other looks at me.

Spenta

(Replying to a letter*)

O beauty of a soul that shall not be
Beheld or held on earth—O little one
That was not made for man, that man can see
Not well 'neath this great veil, for there is none
That shall e'er walk where thou dost tread
Alone where angels move, where seraphim
But flutter where frail flesh to Godhead wed
Lies at this door locked e'en to cherubim . . .
O Tabernacle, tent of th'Ancient Day,
The Sun that comes again to run His course,
Where will be heard again what passed this way
'Tween gaze and gaze from woman's last resource?
O! being made to love, of loving made,
Burn, burn, sweet flame; die well, spent little maid.

*From an enclosed nun.

Before the Shroud
(image, recalling pilgrimage)

O light too bright for retina and sight,
'Yond gaze of burning seraph—matter strong
With shining where electrons puzzle quite
At what came in their midst: high rayons long
With leaps from some strange dark that left a mark
Upon a map, a napkin of small worth
At whose loud stain the æons all here hark,
For here doth stand the hand that planned the Earth.
O! morsel of high Wisdom, wounded limb
And gashed and staggered Godhead, looking wan
And pallid where the light of all lay dim:
I stand upon a rag of ragged man,
And I behold the eye that holds the years,
The brain that in a pain Hell's dungeons sears.

Is this happening?

(First Tridentine Mass*)

And can it be that sound as soft as breath
May work a deed so great? A miracle,
Can it upon a whisper stand, that saith
What oft was said before? A particle,
That hears a magic pulse that travelled here
Upon this old, old stone, 'neath this same sun
As often as it rose, though it appear
To heed not what is said, is it undone . . . ?
O! Majesty that walks a syllable
And bids me twice, thrice, bow and bend the knee
As ages once knew well! How gullible
Is Intellect grown wild, that smiled to be
For ever free from this, high rubric told
To lie in peace with yesteryear now old . . .

*20/7, in the Carolingian chapel.

Beyond the veil
(letter from a nun)

What heavy loads are borne by little leaves
That know not what they move nor what they stir
In their becalmed unfolding: what weight heaves
The pen inanimate where meanings were
The all that moved the air there where no sound
Was heard or word crossed silent lip, where tears
Turned softly into ink; what thinking found
A way to be condensed and sensed by ears—
Not made of coil and tympan, but of this
Thin matter of a soul, where echoes find
A space wherein to ring! Nor e'er a kiss
Was made of such embrace, for here behind
Some lines not even writ, I see, I see
A very being that looks out to me.

For the world you are nobody
(but for somebody you are the world)

Il mondo non esiste, non è qui
Se non in te, se non nell'anima
Che vede tutto, crede tutto—sì,
E vuole solo questa verità
Che sei. Se sei in verità, sei tu
La vita di un'altra: non si ha
Né luce né bellezza dove fu
Un'ora che sarà, sempre sarà,
Perché in quella ora eri lì
Ad essere, ben essere. Sarai
Domani e domani . . . E' così,
La traccia che domani lascerai:
La vita che t'invita, anima,
Ad esser due volte anima.

Una pioggia di lacrime
(alla partenza dell'Arca)

There are some drops too heavy for the world,
Some molecules not made of pow'rs that be
Of matter bound, in soundless orbit hurled
Upon a proton core charged heavily:
There are some sounds that words may not contain,
Some particles of soul that know a way
To come and go there where a little pain
Did find a way to be and nothing say.
There are, my friends, some meanings that stand ill
Upon a syllable, for we are not
Found all within a sound, and we stand still
With little but a trickle ne'er forgot,
To say what matters most, for most of all
We are when we are globules very small.

Questi sono i miei angeli

(Étienne, 10 ans, Louis, 12 ans)

Ô petit être, fait pour être un saint,
Un saint très saint, un saint peut-être un jour
À nommer à l'autel, là où ce pain
Porté par tes deux mains sera toujours
Le centre de ce monde: l'univers
De cette enfance heureuse n'est pas loin
De ce demain des âges que ces vers
Et ces syllabes d'homme tiennent moins—
Moins bien que toi, enfant, moins bien que toi,
Qui connais par éclairs, qui connais tout
En clarté qui sait voir sans autre loi
Sinon la loi du simple rendez-vous
Donné par deux regards, car ici-bas
L'enfant enfreint souvent tout l'Au-delà.

Maria Assunta

(A full church, and a street full of bread and wine)

Good brazen souls baked by meridian heat
And hardened by the Tuscan hammer, red
With sickle and free wine, on this morn meet
The Master that beneath the winepress bled
To wash the luxury of passion strong
That long holds man from God . . . And you, fair dames
That wear these colours bright and calmly throng
These ancient forecourts still, and fan the flames
Of August's canigule with placid cool
And calm of deft ventaglio waved with ease
Through sermon and high prayer, and weigh the fool
That sweats and struts awhile that he may please
The gaze of but a village all forgot:
|I'll save you yet, stray flock, for you're my lot.

(First festive Mass in the village)

220

Fontgombault

O! beauty ever old and ever new,
And standing yet upon the world that turns
Too quickly as it goes—this mystic view
Of glory and of majesty that burns
'Neath cherub wing, where seraph all of fire
'Mid long trisagion veils ardent gaze
And stands where man walks on, and high'r and high'r
Lifts o'er the world a chalice all ablaze . . .
O! mystery where history is all
Attentive to a word not even heard,
In utt'ring thus a syllable so small,
I know that much in stillness such has stirred:
I know, my God, that man has left behind
Much beauty that no dawn again shall find.

(After preaching retreat and mastering Tridentine rite)

Surprise
(the fare to Dublin and to Medugorje)

There is a goodness yet upon the earth,
And angel matter that is made of this,
Fair beauty never wed, sweet gentle mirth
And happiness unknown that all did miss:
There is a kindness here that shall not be
Well felt as't could have been, as kindness might
By kindness be repaid, and none shall see
What here is known alone by angel light.
But all in Ellen's name is made of Thee,
Good Master and fond King, for madness came
From never other source, and mystery
Of giving 'yond control bears well the name
Of Godhead in small breasts hid silently,
And maids are mothers yet; were made to be.

Power

There are strange things at work in little sounds,
And molecules are moulded at a word
By Him that bade them be, and 'tween the bounds
Held by short syllables enough is heard
To ratify and cleanse—alas, nay and
To send to endless drifting where no Blood
May touch again the soul that on this land
A little moment little thinking stood . . .
O Master, here I know I hold Thee well,
For 'twas for aye Thy bidding that this be.
Lead on, O Priest Eternal, for 'tis Hell
Itself Thou'dst have me quench: Eternity
Stands on a hand and tongue, and we are one
In murmured whispers where 'tis done, 'tis done.

(After singing High Mass, preaching, and confessing)

Such trust

To love and be well loved is to be well
Upon a lonely land, a lonely earth
That coils a heedless orb, where none may tell
What one alone may be, what one is worth,
For worth he is to none as unto one
For whom he is worth all—yet, Master, nay,
This should not be, and e'en a little nun
May grow too great in vision's magic ray.
O! virgins hid, hide well your pow'r to please,
For love is not for us, where others roam
A land where hand and hand may probe and tease,
And living can of fondling make a home.
For home below is none, and we shall be
Unknown, unseen, e'en should we something see.

Shot

(by tourist cameras)

To be alone again, to be alone
With Thee, my Friend, my only friend, and end
The noisome pestilence that heavy stone
Draws from the ends of earth—nay, to befriend
As once before a Godhead hid and veiled
In but a flicker standing in the night
Where much is burned at will, and to be railed
Again 'neath strength and length of iron's might:
This would be dungeon sweet. O! cell! O! cell!
Why did I thee so flee, to be all ill
With freedom hardly hemmed, where e'en a bell
Calls all and sundry here, where none is still
With stillness of a God, where still is felt
What once was known where none else came and knelt?

(Recalling 8/9/76, Sélignac)

Medugorje
(after hearing many confessions*)

A word is but a wave, that yet, when heard,
Can touch and hold a soul: the whole of man
Lies on a syllable, and oft is stirred
A depth unreached where once much venom ran.
But till this hour the pow'r of this strange sound
Of healing and unbinding I knew not,
And what in this high whisper was unbound
In depth of Hell I had awhile forgot.
For Godhead passed this way upon this night,
Nor did mere tears flow here: a miracle
Awaited one short breath, and heat and might
A soul and body smote—a particle
Of Grace all tangent came and passed this way,
And robbed a little soul of light of day.

*During one of these a penitent fell
to the floor at the last word of absolution

Grace alone is bold

To know that we are loved and wanted here
Upon this land we tread, to know that one
All hid from this wide world is very near,
And that a monk's lone heart a little nun
Can hold, enfold, and hard by Godhead bear
In dead of night's long watching—that a soul
Another soul can see, that beauty fair,
Ne'er seen by e'er an eye of gazing foul,
Amazing sounds can send, and bend the will
Not unto thoughts but to delights all made
Of resting there where nests no carnal thrill
But only ancient Love: 'tis love afraid
No more to own a name, for shame came not
Upon this page of feelings long forgot.

An adoring angel

To read again is to be doubly moved
By what did stir awhile, to be twiced warmed
By one stray beam that shone, to feel yet loved
Long after what was writ by hours was calmed
And left upon the page that ages not
As quickly as our thoughts: 'tis there to walk
Again with Yesterday today forgot,
And with a lost caught echo yet to talk.
'Tis to be here, my friend, where thou shalt be
Unfurrowed by old lines, for lines like these
Are made of moving soul, and this I see
Is heard for evermore, and sounds that please
Stroke not the ear, but th'years that lie ahead,
And two lie less alone 'neath sound unsaid.

Altar

(of St Maximilian Kolbe's first Mass)

Thou didst bid be, good Saint, what shall here be
Tomorrow on this stone, this place thine own,
Where on a day of days eternity
Stood for a moment still: 'twas here 'twas known,
The myst'ry hist'ry ne'er unmade, the hour
Of passing chargèd sounds, of unbound rays
Magnetic, energetic where a pow'r
Here crossed and tossed the laws of ancient days.
O hail! high morn, high dawn here long, long sighed,
And hail! true Body made of syllable
And whisper heard before; hail! friend that cried,
Hid angel that prayed well, for terrible
Indeed the deed that bid not be this mark,
And 'twould not be, did God well Satan hark.

Ada, ora pro me
(End of thesis, and of letter to Chartreuse)

A heavy load of thinking lies upon
A wad of leaves compressed: here heaves a sigh
A breast that on a thought thought on and on,
And heard the voices that touch yet the eye.
Tomorrow this will go and doctor hours
Or be rejected yet and call for more,
For plumes of men are feathered yet by pow'rs
Of man's own kind, that oft unkindness bore . . .
And this swift sheet, this other softly sent
Into the old unknown, known far too well
To be forgotten quite, there as it went
To western Gallic skies, did it yet tell
Enough to bring again all that can be
The home of doctors doctored, Saint, by thee?

Digit

A pulse to catch a second as it goes
Upon its ancient way; a day held still
Till onward too it moves, there where nought shows
The way it once did come; a passing, till
A passage here is writ for evermore
Upon old Chronos' script, where tipped each day
Into the many more that once of yore
Had shone a while, a little while, for aye . . .
O! thing that has no name, commodity
The same through seconds foul and moments fair,
Here linger in my hand: eternity
Is made perhaps of thee. Two rayons there
I see upon the hours that lie ahead:
But one well poised, and one for e'er unsaid.

(Setting clock given by Dolgellau Carmel after
High Mass, and pondering on the Charterhouse.)

Nous nous retrouverons—sur les nuées

Un jour, un autre, encore un autre jour
Tout fait de ce qui passe, et ce qui fut
Demain sera encore: encor toujours
Hier sera cet Aujourd'hui vécu . . .
Mais vous, mes sœurs—mes sœurs du grand Hier
Qui, ici, vit encore—où serez-vous
Quand Demain passera? Ce lieu si cher
Connaîtra-t-il alors ces sons si doux?
Ô joie si triste! Jamais dans la nuit
Fut connue telle lampe, car ce feu,
Où meurt un lourd Passé sans moindre bruit,
M'attire à m'approcher de ce saint lieu . . .
Car ce qui fut sera et durera
Là où ce long Hier nous cachera.

(Mon anniversaire, la nuit, pendant la retraite
chez les Victimes du Sacré-Cœur, Marseille,
durant la psalmodie des Matines)

Veiled

(and hidden by two grilles)

O souls made all of love, O souls of fire,
Fair seraphim unseen that hover high
And nigh to Godhead's height, high, highest quire
Of maidens made of God, beam where no cry
Of human kind may reach, and teach me all
That need be known on earth, here where your light
Burns softly on and on, where droplets small
Of woman kind's fair all die in the night.
O! suff'ring never heard, O! word made known
To none but Him the King, O! body poured
Into a place of pain, where nought was shown
To any that came by—here is adored
With limb and hurting limb what is not seen,
And I have stood 'neath sounds of having been.

(After preaching and celebrating in old rite for the
Victims of the Sacred Heart)

233

Binding
(thesis)

When we have gone, a word upon a page
Perhaps will linger on, and we shall be
No more a ray of vision that of age
Is made and soon unmade: eternity
Lies only 'yond the grave, yet we wave on
A message more or two where some may come
Again perhaps upon this way where shone
A glister of a Now long Then become.
For Then lies hard herein, and we may know
A moment doubly weighed where once it went
Into the æons' night a light to show
To one to come again. For much was sent
Across the chasmic years across a line,
A little line all wired of thinking fine.

(Rome)

Retreat
(and after preaching four)

This will be time ahead, this will be life,
The rhythm of the moments as they go,
With some thus set apart. A little strife,
And we shall be no more, nor shall one know
The path that once was trod, for nevermore
Shall footsteps come this way, and pain that came
Shall come no more where pains were known before,
For onward shall this orb turn on the same.
Yet I am well, good Master, in this task
Of calling from the shores of Evermore:
To linger by old rayons, and to bask
A lengthy while 'mid waves of distant yore
Is to be but a mystagog—to be
A little Beatrice on Eternity.

(Abbey)

235

All need not be

O! wonder of it all, that there are hours
Not all of others made—that there can be
In being doubly well, therein where pow'rs
Of soul move all alone, a mystery
All, all of nothing made, for nothing more
Than nothing finely made is needed here
For meeting once again a sound of yore
Left be upon a day and buried near:
For we are near again to what we are
And were awhile before when more alone
With nothing much but such as shall not mar
The form of emptiness in fulness known.
For sound is bound all, all of Meaning small,
Too small to be oft shattered by a call.

(In retreat)

Offeren San Piws V

Ai dyma'r geiriau glywyd gynt un dydd,
A dyddiau lawer gyda'r wawr a fu
Yn torri ar ein tir? Ai gwir y ffydd,
Y ffydd ddi-sail a'i sail yn fudan su—
Y sibrwd mân di-sain a glywyd gynt
Fel heddiw'n troi elfennau dan hen wyrth?
Oes, mae sain, atsain engyl yn y gwynt
Lle chwelir ag ond sill hen efydd Byrth.
O! Gwpan Hen!—dan wên merthyri fry
A waedodd er dy fwyn! O! ddefod gain,
A ddysgwyd gan fyrdd sant! Mae yma lu
Yn troedio uwch fy mhen. Na, sisial main
A dynn ar nef y nef, a dyma Ef
Yn sefyll yn fy llaw heb lais na llef.

(Noswyl San John Roberts)

The art of listening

When I behold the breath of many days
That was on nothing spent, when I pay heed
To sounds sent to the void, when I the rays
Of might see t'ward the night cast without need,
Then am I sad to see what had to be
Upon a moment lost, where tossed was all
That was within without, for now I see
What mighty matters move on movements small.
O Master, all is here: 'tis here the light
Wherein alone Thou'lt hide, for other than
The space 'twixt lip and lip is nothing quite
As wide as this that hides the whole of man.
We are unblest in messages ill sent,
For in much sound was found not much well meant.

(In retreat)

Astud, o flaen y gwirfod

(ar ôl Offeren Ladin ddistaw)

Y mae i eiriau weithiau ormod sain,
Ac yn ein holl leferydd osteg trai.
Ond gwn, wir Dduw, am lef, am adlef mân
Sydd uchaf oll, cans oll na hyn sydd lai.
Y lleiaf oll o'r synau sydd yn bod
Yw gwyrth ynganiad dyn, a Duw a wêl
Y gwir a ddeil heb gymorth sain na nod,
Cans nodwyd enaid â diddiflan sêl.
Y mae, dan drem yr Hen Ddihenydd, le
I fod, i fod yn ddim ond bod a fydd
Yn bod lle mae, yn bod lle mae Efe,
Yn agos at y Bod yn unig sydd.
Ac nid yw'n bod greadur yn y byd
Fel un a ŵyr yn llwyr y synau mud.

(San John Roberts, merthyr yr Aberth)

Last Saturday in the cloister
(of the Angelicum)

Beginnings have long endings upon earth,
And times that lingered whiles must onward move.
The sounds of merry voices, where old mirth
Of ancient youth was heard again, the love
Of angel veils that found a friend must end,
And unto stern long chilling slowly turn,
For cloister unto cloister here does send
A little flame that learns well tamed to burn.
O! halcyon days, where hope of morrows bright
Drove pen and pulpèd brain, where onward go
The sparks of wit into a long dimmed night
Made all of growing old, bid one here grow
Not unto frigid matter having been,
But to a distant dream that once was seen.

Hôtelier

(à partir du mois de février)

'Tis said that angels came and angels went
In humnan rags through these monastic inns,
That Christ made flesh again was hither sent
Unto these hostels of dim origins . . .
O ancient art of welcoming, be warm
As in the mediæval night, where feet
Trudged o'er these heights in blizzard and through storm
To find a homely face, a place of heat.
O! charge obscure, yet cure to many pains,
Small bridge 'tween world and cloister, I thee take
With hands outheld, for though nought hence retains
My feet in this sweet cell, I well shall make
Of necessaries virtue, for a while,
For much old warmth wrapped wand'rers with a smile.

(After being told the news)

241

Ihr wißt nicht was morgen sein wird*

There is no knowing what the morrow brings
Upon the wings of dawn; there is no hour
That knows another's shape, and little things
Today upon Tomorrow wield much pow'r,
For though a dream be bright upon the night
That broods on days to come, its light when seen
May yet be doubly wan, for man's full might
Is might that might have been and not have been . . .
O Morrow, burn yet brightly in the sky
Of Hope that spins the earth, for mirth is yet
In but a sparkle held, and rhythms high
Move in Youth's early dance ere sunlight set
Upon a day or two too quickly burnt,
For fairer is the morn than eves aye learnt.

*Js 4:14

Virgin*

O virgin bright, held tightly by the King
Beyond the night of man—where none may come
Save One alone for whom such angels sing
As were not kown on earth—build here thy home
Of grille and veil well girt, and walk along
The corridors of time to where no hour
May trouble yet the calm of this sweet song
That shall have been once sung in frail youth's flow'r.
O! littleness so huge and never held
By aught of human kind, this highest flame
Of madness that cast all, that all withheld
Upon a sheet, a mark, a dark ink's name—
I cannot look upon this sacrifice,
For here a lamb I leave to Paradise.

(After yesterday's profession
of four from Lecceto)

*Ap 14:4

243

Veilleuse qui meurt
(Victime du Sacré-Cœur)

Allez, ma sœur, allez dans l'Au-delà
Si longtemps attendu, et entrevu
Devant ces portes closes qui, tout bas,
Nous disent leur secret, car il a plu
À l'Hôte de l'autel où tant d'amour
A été répandu, de voiler bien
L'Aurore qui nous guête, car le jour
Qui point à l'horizon, ce point de rien,
Cette heure, cet atome fait de temps,
Contient les continents d'éternité
Où luit le demain de ce long printemps
Qu'ici, ma sœur, vous avez sacrifié . . .
Là où vous giserez, une heure éteinte:
Là sera, frêle mèche, l'Heure atteinte.

Eve of St Agnes*

O purest virgin, vested for a King
And crowned with thorns He bore, shine brightly on:
Here ever ever more thy soft lay sing
With chords of greenest youth, till days be gone
To fullest age of womanhood unused,
And this our novice song be but a dream
Of flame and flame once shared, where two had mused
Upon the dim eve's form at dawn's first gleam.
Recall, unplucked hid petal of the Lord
Who walks a garden closed, how close was Might,
Made all of His strange pow'r, in this thy word
Not uttered but well sent and captured quite
In pores that held His all, for smallest bliss
Did move from chrismèd hands to thy soft kiss.

*After blessing Michela—now Sr Maria Michela Chiara
della Santissima Trinità—through narrow confines.

Chartreuse
(Sélignac, framed)

When I behold the past that never was,
Yet can perhaps still be, when I behold
The days that dawned where dawning ever has
A way to dawn again, when I here hold
Tomorrow in my little hand, where stands
The pow'r to bid yet be or bid not be
An hour full small, all full of other lands
That dangle thinly o'er Eternity—
When, when, I say, I hold the morrow yet
Upon a pulse of willing, that can bring
For e'er again what ne'er I can forget,
Then something deeply hurt yet 'gins to sing
A little where a song was known, well known,
For God and man were made to be alone.

Replacing volumes
(in the library)

Rest now in peace, good books, my quiet friends
That have without aught utt'ring all well taught
In these months academic, for here ends
A moon or two that æons old hath caught.
I did peruse and wander through a land
Made all of leaves so thin and densely packed,
While having none to guide me but this hand
Stretched from beyond the grave where thought lay stacked.
For heavily combined were thinking forms
That carried this high load of chargèd Mind,
And, though they softly lie, the gath'ring storms
Of wanting what they say leaves not behind
The little child still wild with wanting this
High place that this pen knew that drew this bliss.

Allumé
(ayant reçu les charges)*

Je veux, je veux, à jamais je le veux,
Car vouloir, c'est tout pouvoir ici-bas,
Et en me donnant ainsi par ce vœu
Je vis du vieux Voulu de l'Au-delà.
Ô Maître de ce jour en son déclin
Depuis son origine auprès de Toi,
Ancien des jours, Tu lis bien ce destin
Tracé devant Ta Face et sous Ta loi.
Tu vois, et Tu as vu, et souvent lu,
En encre noire, en encre indélébile,
Irréversible, drue, ce qu'il a plu
À Ton roseau d'écrire en scribe habile.
Car ce qu'un jour à l'autre dictera
Fut fait d'un point qui sera et sera . . .

(Présentation)

*Sacristain, hôtelier

נדי סֹפַֿרְתָה אָתָה

(. . . und das plötzlich, in einem Augenblick*)

O Lord of all that was, was ever, ever all
That was aye seen as having to have been
Tomorrow yesterday: this ray so small
Upon a candle spent and quickly seen
To be no more is more than meets the eye,
For 'tis the voice of all that shall not be
Tomorrow here again, for here am I
Adance in this that burns Eternity.
O light upon the night that heavily
Draws fair and festered sin to where mankind
Would go while there's yet heat, I readily
Will die if dying is the Master's mind.
For I behold in holding this short wick
The measure of this twinkled Augenblick.

Candlemas

(after receiving charge of

sacrist and guestmaster.)

*1 Cor 15: 52

נדי ספרתה אָתָה: Peregrinationes meas tu numerasti (Ps 56, 9).

A new confessional
(many years old)

I clean what shall clean all that in a man
And womankind is spread, for yesterday
Still travels through this grille, and no age can
Much alter what is here and came this way:
I here recall what secrets could be heard
But once upon this earth; I hear, I hear
And see the liquid sins that in a word
Did melt and trickle down when grace was near.
I see again the beauty of a soul,
The uggliness of some, the peace withheld,
For that the will was not, and that the whole
Would still be held awhile, for I beheld,
Here set 'tween Heav'n and Earth, full foul fair things,
For each that knelt I felt, where brimstone clings.

Penmon

(Writing to Bishop Morgan, Tanya, Dylan, and
Gwilym)

O come again, fair moon that shone before
On Erin and on Wales, land of our song,
Land of our yesterdays, where many more
Once trod the acres that to Heav'n belong . . .
There is across the sea a place for me
To be one day again, my God, I know,
For though there sigh much that bids calmly be
A hermit hid and clad, it is not so:
The Will that holds all sway shows not the way
To ope this door again, but, groping still,
I shall move on a day, another day,
Until another yet the gentle thrill
Of knowing Home again, of hearing sound
Once heard before, be once more some day found.

(Bd Hugh, first Abbot of Prémontré)

O light!

O! light, O! blessed Trinity,
O! might, O! primal Unity,
This fiery sun now goes its way;
In these our hearts shed now Thy ray.

To Thee we sang with rays of dawn,
To Thee this evening praise be borne:
A prostrate glory now receive,
O! glory of no age, no eve.

To God the Father, glory be,
To God the Son, eternally,
With Paraclete, the Spirit blest,
Trisagion sung without rest.

Amen.

(Melody: *O lux beata*)

(After singing Mass,
facing the rising sun)

Fourteenth
(Holy Mass for a holy nun)

O virgin pure, that penned a Valentine,
What can this mean, that thou shouldst yearn to be
Remembered here on earth, that thoughts of mine
Should travel 'cross the skies and, heard by thee,
Tap yet upon a little chord within
Not wholly snapped, where woman kind knows not
The art of death? For though there be no sin
Upon this page, I see a rage forgot . . .
O little soul, so far from any man,
What bid thee call, what bade thee leave a word
To end a missive bland, a message wan,
With but a phrase whose massive rays were heard?
Fair angel never seen and never known,
I know thee well, for I too walked alone.

A secret

(Three wise monkeys:
See-naught, Hear-naught, Say-naught)

A secret word was heard upon an hour
Made soft by its own coming: but a sound
Made all of hearing well and knowing pow'r
In rays of thought was in a moment found,
And 'twas enough to still a clamour vast
That shall not be, that need not be, that shall
Not ever, ever be, for at the last
We can yet die as this wise animal.
Much need not be, I see, much need not be,
And moments linger long when given room
To be and to be well, for, Lord, I see
That all is here, for here is very doom
Or bliss, sweet bliss, for this, the all of all,
Is made of but one trick huge, hugely small.

(Shrove Tuesday)

Letter from the Grande Chartreuse

I will return to Paradise; I will,
If this be giv'n again: a little word,
A nod of God on high, a sign can still
For aye the years disturbed. One mark yet heard
Upon the silent page can open wide
The skies for evermore and lock the door
Of sound and rumour high, there where to hide
Again would be to heed fond sounds of yore.
O Master, call again, and let me come
To this fair prison dark where there is light
Enough to see the sight of this old home
Where lover spoke to Lover in the night.
Bid, gentle Lord, a gentle, gentle pen
But turn this little key for aye from men.

(Devising letter for Dom Isidore)

After not looking
(at a film)

The heart is still when sound is bound to be
Away from where we are, for we are there
But then when all is heard, and we well see
But when there is but list'ning in the air.
O King of Æons long and silent Time,
That marches slowly on 'neath these Thy feet
That tapped this way before, a little chime
Bids twice think on the use of this small beat.
For moment speaks of moment in the dark,
And carries weight in mem'ry's clouded cell,
For ruffled is the mind that bid this mark
Of din and heaviness here inward dwell.
And I can hear Thy shuffling, when a sound
Is by a little absence deftly bound.

(Shrove Tuesday)

Request

There is upon a page an age to be
Or not to be again, a time to come,
A moment turned to ancient history
For ever in my home, my only home,
Or suff'ring brought again and wrought again
In man's unthinking voice left upon this
The whiteness of a leaf made but of pain,
Or made perhaps, who knows, of cravèd bliss—
The all lies upon this, the all, the all
Can hold Tomorrow well or bid it sigh
For that it never came, and inches small
Contain a continent where moments lie . . .
O! hurt of a huge Nay, come not this way,
Or better 'twere to ink not this dark day.

(St Joseph)

Awake
(first funeral)

Our moments have an ending upon earth,
And hours here long are but a song to be
Once sung upon this stage, yet they are worth
The markèd weight of ancient History
That can but be, that can but never change—
No more than this ghost's form that that 'gins to rest
Upon frail laurels gained all 'neath the range
Of brittle seconds setting 'yond the West.
O! sound of æons' calm, that waited long
For this last child, that wildly cried a day,
Yawn on upon this dream, for 'tis the gong
Of unmistaken waking strikes for aye.
And we are made to be what we have made
Of moments old once told and ever weighed.

(Easter Monday)

Μηδέν 'άγαν
(Ne quid nimis)

There is a mystery in history,
A secret never found, yet loudly heard
By any that will hark, for hurriedly
Hell-bound did Man walk on past this one word
That could have stilled all others and remained
Enough to hold the world, for hurled was all
Into a vortex fraught where naught was gained
But Heaviness there where enough were small.
O! joy too late beheld! I see, I see
A way to better be, if this be held
By all the hold of being, for, to be,
'Tis best to rest with blessedness beheld,
And pass not to another: it is this,
To tremble once, but once, for short is bliss.

Unopened
(letter from Dom Isidore)

What lies within? What lies within? What hours
Lie sealed in this slim space? What pace will these
Now tap as onward roll the mighty pow'rs
Of chimes that time our all? What gentle breeze
Or blast do I unfold and boldly read?
A sound here pounds within at this thin wall,
And soon 'twill reach my innards, that will feed
For ever on its shape beyond recall.
For here the æons lie, and calmly lie,
Awaiting their soft turn, for go they shall
The way by this script marked, for matter high
With Destiny aye inked is linked withal,
And I behold hid 'neath a sealèd sound
A gash or bliss to cosmic years e'er wound.

Words electric
(from Mount Tabor)

O little child, forgotten and forlorn,
Will this yet happen, that thou bid'st here be?
The dark of starkest night, will it the dawn
Of long encounter blest one day yet see?
Will day give in to day where noise of man
May cloud no more the earth? Will night be made
For more than light can hold? Will wanting fan
The fire of wanting more what this sound bade?
O force of happenings unhappened well
And torn to shreds in noised calamity,
Canst yet restitch th'unravellings of Hell
That blotched the tracèd map of History?
O Amma, will this be? Can it yet come?
Will those two lonely eyes be light of Home?

Pressed
by Taboric rays)

To know that we are wanted upon earth
Within but one veiled breast; that there are hours
Made empty that wait yet; that one is worth
The world for one small soul; that all the pow'rs
Of wanting much are such as make us be
No longer unaware, but ever there
In mind's regard, till narded sense may see
Again a gaze once fond, a face once fair:
'Tis to be touched not by the hand of man
But Godhead that traced all, for calling here
'Neath pulse of ink's soft pull is fulness wan
With wanting where came nought but oft a tear.
For to be wanted is to be a soul,
A pinèd spectre of a mind unwhole.

An eve all fraught
(with memories four years old)

It is the hour, the day, that brought strange things
Awhile this way, for days that day stood still
For but a season, yet the hours have wings
And bear us onward where the morrow will
Bid moments ever go, for we know not
The pow'r of but a moment over all,
And what might yet have been the fairest lot
Of two was cast aside with thinkings small.
The hour that strikes again, will't bring me home
To yesterday's long hope, will something move
Yet all the cogs and trappings that yet come
'Twixt what we know and what we know to love?
Will stillness come again to this loud world
That was, irenic angel, at thee hurled?

Virgin mother

(what pain was caused. ..)

When I behold the night and what therein
Moves onward in the dark; when I behold
Beneath the noonday sun the form of sin
That clouds the vision in a thought too bold;
When I see well that Hell is all agog
At what it yet can do; when through and through
I see how yet to shift each wheel and cog
Of engines beaureaucratic and let woo
A sigh heard from afar,a heart, a soul
And meaning made of Sense that hath a name,
I cry aloud upon the darkness foul
That came upon a morn, for here the same
There stands before my eyes a little one
That pow'r yet wields to turn the morrow's sun.

Midsummer night redreamt

O mother of a home where I was born
Beneath a western star, to be, to be
Afar from being much, from being worn
By being many things, shall we yet see
A day whereon again a door shall clap
Upon the noisome sound of touring bands
Of hominides ungraced, and will the lap
Of virginal fond care from distant lands
Receive again a child defiled by men
Who tread too loudly in the home of God,
And know not where they stand? Will yearning then
Be turned to holding e'er a bliss once trod
By two who knew a little of a thing
That through a rage and silence strange doth cling?

Κρίσις

O glory of a grace yet standing there,
Upon the morrow dangling, handle well
The syllables that travel in the air
And hold the pow'r to bless or foul in Hell.
This is the danger of a great demand
By one not free to choose, and losing all
In lost Eternity lies hand in hand
With gaining Heav'n twice o'er in but a call.
For Solitude's soft voice is high anon,
And I see well two eyes that wept awhile
For Yesterday's return, yet here upon
A sound is found a curse bound e'er to style
The noise of days unborn, or yet again
A ray to bend and mend the æons' pain.

Darlun

(Anti Lisa)

Y mae i fudan lun ryw drydan lef
Na ŵyr y glust, a thila ddu a gwyn
Ddeil eto bwysau un: yn entrych Nef
Yr hoff, hoff wên a welir sydd fan hyn
Yn dawel a di-gnawd, cans ffawd a roes
Eiliedyn brau ar gof a chadw hir,
A hwy fydd einioes llun na'r wedd a droes
Dan rith pelydryn yn anhydrin wir.
O! greulon ddyfais Dyn, ni wyddost di
Dy allu ar wneuthurwr orig hen
A saif am byth lle sefaist: drosom ni
Deil nod a sêl dy drem, a bregus wên
Am oesoedd ddenfyn eto haul a fu,
Fu unwaith, orig fer, mor annwyl gu.

Monte Oliveto
(revisited)

O place wherein a Face shone brightly well
Ere beams came from on high—O! little land
Where Godhead trod with man, and very Hell
Cringed all to see a mischief in a hand
Of pow'r and Pontiff high—O! sigh once heard
Within a breast by angels watched and held
Hard by the Master's waiting for a word
In years and tears too long hard, hard withheld:
I walk again where yesterday was high
With knowing of a God whose nod was all
That mattered at the last, for blasted lie
The botchings of high fiends in soft a call
Upon a morrow waiting yesterday
Here, here, fond Olivet, 'cross Nay and Nay.

Breuddwyd

(Llythyr gan yr Esgob Edwin)

A ddown yn ôl i'r parthau tyner hyn
Lle buom gynt, lle bu ein hynt yn rhwydd,
Lle bu hen oriau bychain eto'n wyn
Heb bwysau oed, heb grych a rhych hir swydd—
A welwn eto'r erwau lle bu swyn
A sain Yfory'n gân ar wawr ein dydd,
Pan dreodiem dir gwir freuddwyd eto'n fwyn
Ei lliw a'i lledrith cyn dwyn rhithiau prudd?
A wawria eto dros ganghellau hen
Ein llannau bychain, lle bu gwyrth rhy fawr
At frau amgyffred dyn, ryw ddwyfol wên
Nas diffydd unrhyw nos—os diffodd sydd
I dân canrifoedd hen, i wên gwir ffydd?

Luana
(«Ci sono pocchi che ne escono».)

When I behold the light that in a night
Was lost in wanting much, in wanting such
As wanting will not wait; when fairest sight
Made sightless once, made tight by but a clutch—
Not e'en of holding held, but all of this
High bliss of molecules—is lit again,
And truth is said in but a simple kiss:
Then there is hope again upon the earth
Where pleasure need not have a measure thus
As leaps a mega range, for gentlest mirth
Came not with hottest prickings that held us
Upon a jet of whetted ecstasy
All needled by a need that need not be.

Too late

(«Devo andare in fondo della campagna
a benedire un morto».)

The time is long and distance evermore
Shall be 'tween what we are and what we were
Yet yesterday, yet yesterhour, that saw
The sawing of all time, for what did stir,
Good soul now e'ermore gone to bygone age
Upon a moment small that called the all
To ordering anon, did stir one page
That for all time is turned beyond recall.
O hominide too huge to lie unknown
In but a common tomb, a womb there is
No more to hide thee from the blast now shown
To be the all that is, unless 'tbe His
That sparked thee, little splinter of a star
Gone on to wander, wonder where days are.

Hope
(of founding)

Hail, Poltergeist, whose spirit walks the air
Electric, wherein wave on technic wave
Aspark with marks unseen lurk densely there
Upon a molecule that bids us rave
Together 'cross the miles! What smiles are these,
Old friend, whose end had been long told, whose mind
Lay long unread? What dead man walks the seas
Of moments once shared well and left behind?
Hail, hail, fond Ghost; come hither, to this dream
Cast on old Erin's shore, where days before
Were happy and were new, and if this gleam
Be given from on high, we'll push this door
A little, little more till it be ours,
For ghost with ghost well joists with spectred hours.

(After receiving Fr Benedict's E-mail)

272

Mam

Beth ydyw lliw ar fudan femrwn brau
Na ddeil ei dir yfory, na fydd mwy
Yn ddim ond mymryn megis briwsion clau
Hen foleciwlau'r byd sy'n teithio trwy
Eonau maith yr oes? Nid oes fan hyn
Ond dernyn o hen beth, ond plethwaith sydd
Ar gelloedd gwyn yr hud a saif yn syn
Ar gof a chadw hir a eto fydd:
Yfory saif yr awr sy'n awr yn troi
Yn ôl i echdoe pell, a gwell, mi wn,
Yw'r orig fechan hon sydd eto'n cloi
Cyfarwydd wên hen wyneb ar glawr hwn
O rith a erys—na, nid byth, ond dro,
Ond olaf dro—na machlud hir y gro.

Diffoddwyd

(gwên llun Anti Mair)

Y mae i fudan lun ryw dawel lef
Na ŵyr y glust; y mae i lygad hen
A gaeodd am hir hun, belydryn Nef
A welir lle y mae; y mae i wên
Gyfarwydd na ddaw mwy, oleuni brau
A saif ar fregys ddalen eto'n glir
Yfory eto dro, a'r hyn a wnai
Y wyneb cu, fe'i gwna mewn arall dir.
Cans er ond orig yw ein gwên a'n cân,
Y mae i rai ryw seiniau eto ddaw
Yn ôl, yn ôl o bell, a geiriau mân
Sydd fawr eu hadlef yn y cof na thaw.
A lle bu rhinwedd etyb rhywbeth dro
I'r wedd a wena'n hir dan hedd y gro.

Come over and help us

What meaneth this, that beck'nings should be seen
Upon the night of distant Macedon?
The light of Egrin once long having been
In Gwalia's dark, has it its last work done?
Or will it burn again, not in our land,
That called us home, but 'hind a Kremlin wall?
This gentle, gentle stretching of a hand
Once known through grille and cloister, dare it call?
Is there yet strength upon a length of wire
To pull a soul asunder and bid come
Away, away to where a fragrant fire
Can sever home and country and bid roam
No more upon a planet where no man
Can love a God as but a woman can?

(Romania calling)

Er gab ihnen Macht über die unreinen Geister
(Mk 6:7, Lutherbibel)

To love a nun is to be none too well,
To chafe 'tween confines all of wanting much
Of such as may not be, for very Hell
Beats loudly in the gentlest, fondest clutch
Hence kindled and thence strangled where it ends,
And where all, all, begins, as 'gan to be
For many once gone on where no more lends
The body its soft hand to ecstasy . . .
Yet I will love a nun, and merrily,
And fear for not a soul, for wholly mine
Is it to hold the bride of God, if warily
I learn to love with love of rays of Thine.
For priested I am all in cherub lands,
And 'tis but Thee I hold in little hands.

(Pondering over Romanian invitation)

Relic

(of St Rita):
"that she may bring you back to us."

O place of grace where many things have been,
And many more shall be, should this become
The way to Paradise, for we have seen,
Sweet sisters of an hour, our ancient home,
The merriment that once was meant to be
In gaze and gaze long held, for here beheld
Again were plains of foulèd destiny.
O peace of mind behind the gates of light
Where virgins walk alone! What here was known
Was known before, and 'fore the hermit's sight
Old vistas fond are visited alone:
For lands once known long stand, unchanged, unchanged,
And never was an exile less estranged.

(Last night of retreat, Romania)

Reclusery

(chapel, St Stephan's Abbey)

Will this yet be, hid Sisters of an age
Gone by, yet known alone 'tween these high walls?
The hours unwrit on Hist'ry's famèd page
A gaze of glory marks, nay, hourly calls:
We are not long upon a lengthy time,
For Yesterday e'er was, now that 'tis not,
And, Sisters that soft sing on th'agèd chime
Unchanged, unchanged, pray yet on this my lot:
For home I'd come, with you, to this far land
Of Solitude hard held, for worlds apart
Are strangers of a noise and those that stand
Upon a hidden beating of a heart
Walled doubly well, for Hell came not this way,
And this old moment came perhaps to stay.

(Augsburg)

Reden ist Silber, Schweigen ist Gold

O Solitude made all of being here
Upon a moment rested – blest fair sound
All of a nothing made: here all is near
And far, far, far away, for we are bound
By words on altars writ, and we may not
As quickly as we came tread yet again
To this far Paradise not quite forgot,
For bliss perhaps on earth is made of pain.
Yet if, good Master, this sweet maiden plea,
That calls to Orient lands, be hither borne
By workings of a gentle Majesty
That waited long on calcule of this morn,
Then bid it be, and I shall crack in peace
The shackels of a noise that shall now cease.

(Augsburg)

Werdet ihr bitten, was ihr wollt...
(Jn 15:7)

'Tis in the pow'r of will to bid e'er be
Or bid not be what we see here before
The forking of all time: Eternity
Lies on a wanting well, a little more,
A little more again, till here be clapped
The bargain with all days to be yet born
'Neath pent an Orient sky, ere they be trapped
Upon a harnessed Fate by great wheels borne.
O Sister of hid pow'r, if pow'r be such
'Tween woman and a God, nod at the skies
And bid this be, for I would gently touch
E'ermore but angels and see in their eyes
The tend'rest rays e'er rendered to a King,
If will by Will be blest in this strange thing.

(Augsburg, before the Bd Sacrament)

Galwad lleian

Y mae i bethau hen eu newydd wedd,
Ond Duw nis diffydd neb, ac Ef fydd Ef
Yfory ac yfory yn Ei hedd,
A saif yn hir yn hen randiroedd Nef.
Y ddoe fe glywyd llais a thyner gân
Y weddi gyfyd byth, a nyth fu hon,
Y gorlan gudd, yn nydd y wiryf lân
Na wybu un ei chroes, i loes pur fron:
Ni welwyd cur a gladdwyd, ni bu sôn
Ar dafod nac ar ddalen am y byd
A oedd yr oll i'r oll a dreiddiai fôn
Noeth Ddyndod a fu yma'n hynod fud.
Ond 'fory daw yn ôl, yn ôl, yn ôl
Am byth, am byth byth bythoedd orig ffôl...

(Lleiandy Tettenweis)

Bewahre deinen Fuß, wenn du zum Haus Gottes gehst, und komm, daß du hörest.
(Eccles 4:17)

There will be time tomorrow to be here,
All here, as yesterday were those whose way
Led ever hitherward, for very near
Is Evermore to but a simple day.
There will be time tomorrow to be all,
All ever, all at one, at all one end,
One end and point of being, and withal
To be no more of all but all a blend.
O virgins that peep hard behind this gate
That these our chrismèd hands ope wide for you,
Teach me to bend the bars of heavy Fate
And leap upon a moment ever true:
For morrows come no more as once they did,
And one, one mighty hour must days all bid.

(St Gertrude's Abbey, Tettenweis)

**Denn wenige Jahr noch, und ich gehe den Wege,
den ich nicht widerkommen werde.**
(Job 16:22)

This is the road whereon a traveller goes
And comes not back to tell the lengthy tale.
The workings of a being no one knows
As it is bid not be, as it e'er fails.
The road is long, where song is heard no more,
And journeys have old endings where we go
Upon Tomorrow's wings, for all before
That Yesterday e'er knew must this hour know.
O! moment weighed and counted, second heaved
By æons ere we were, and heard again
When clapped is our last dangling: here is weaved
The long, long thread of Clotho for a gain
Made of an Evermore that shall not cease
To hurt or to caress in riskèd peace.

                              (In retreat)

Stella a stella differt in claritate
(1 Cor 15:41)

There is a glory in the universe
Unclapped upon the earth, and mirth awaits
The senses never stroked for better, worse
And ever that might be 'twixt wedded fates:
There is and there will be for evermore
A height of knowing and of touching well
The all of calling utmosts that this door
Of tombèd slumber seals o'er Heav'n or Hell.
There is upon an æon Waiting long
Upon a sparkle gained or darkened hours,
And in the silence of a maid's last song
Unheard by man there ran vast cosmic pow'rs.
For star from star shall differ for a day
As bright as this thy night was dark for aye.

> (In retreat, meditating on the Victims of the Sacred
> Heart, one of whom is dying, relatively young.)

It happened

There was a time when never was an hour
Upon the cosmos hanging, when no day
Had dawned upon the morn that ancient pow'r
Might yet bid shine and be, when ever aye
Thick darkness moved aloft and measured well
The distances unmade, and spheres came not
To trouble unborn æons, when e'en Hell
Unsparked yet was ere sprites its dark could plot.
But there was warmth upon unfurling rays
That seared, espied far eves ere stirred a dawn,
For specks of naught were caught beneath a gaze
Of One that looked from ecstasy forlorn
For some scintilla that might happy be
Perhaps, perhaps, should happenings agree.

(Et Verbum caro factum est)

Alpha and Omega

When I behold the sky and whence it came,
Ere moments were, ere stirred dazed Chronos' eyes,
Ere Void had yawned or e'er were giv'n a name,
Or stars had winked across the ancient skies,
Then well I hear the spheres in music high
Upon a yesteryear, a yesterhour
The ways of light yet trav'ling, for here I
Behold the rays once sent by Day's stray pow'r.
And there 'yond Lethe's fondling of old Time
Long set to rest, some blest soft hours to come
Await, awake, for but a little chime
Whereat the all shall rock and call us home.
For but a clap of ticking shall yet bid
Hence aye, aye, trap aught ever Time e'er did.

31/12/99 – 1/1/20
(Millennial second

Here begins the end
(Could you take the noviciate?)

O pain upon the bliss that hurts and hurts
To know that 'twill not come! O home not found
'Mid Sisters of an hour! O phrase that blurts
A life unmade in but a brittle sound!
High charge of highest majesty, come nigh
And mar the æons with what shall not be!
For, Master, Thine's my will, but still a sigh
I ill withhold where bold a virgin's plea.
To love we're born, and, though forlorn I hide
From noise that must abide, I see that Thou
Wouldst have me hide not maidens from the tide
Of emptiness on earth, but mirth bestow
In loving in Thy name, the same, the same,
Some unfledged angels that e'en hither came.

Fire
(Bleeding and burning Host)

O! sight upon the night of human kind,
That saw too well to see, that passed this by
'Neath ecstasy grown great, nay, greatly blind
To particles of Bliss wherein ran high
The energies unknown... Aha! here shown
Is what came nigh upon a day wherein
The Master took my hand – here stands full shown
The matter that soft muttering within
Doth cancel from the cosmos and drive hence
To form a throne for Glory: gory pain
In white of fire, love incandescent, tense
With Being hugely here, again, again
Performs a ghostly trickery, and plays
A game forgot e'en by high technic rays.

(After seeing video of miraculous Host venerated
in Augustinian convent, Los Teques, Venezuela.)

Fuerunt

Upon a day there hangs a day or two
Not made of time, but of long hours gone by
That linger yet, for set in fading hue
Of pigment and of pen, the moments high
But once upon the cosmos where they moved
Are true again a while, a little while,
For though no heart beat yet where these once loved,
There hovers mystery upon a smile.
O faces of our yesteday, what knew
The placid grin that thus withstands the age
That set where your sun set, and what was true
But once in time, that for all time a page
Holds firm for man's long puzzling – what aye more
Remains of pains and ecstasies of yore?

(Castiglione della Pescaia)

289

O purity!

Had I but known how much a nun could mean,
Would I so soon have passed these heavy walls
That hold such mystery? Had I but seen
In catching two glimpsed eyes, what gentle calls
That never found a voice could travel yet
From depth of an abyss where none e'er came
To stir a maiden yearn, would I have let
My hand yet draw the softness of name?
O flickering scintilla kindled still
Where God and man both meet, O virgin spark
Ignited by His priest, release the will
That binds this heavy chain, for e'en the dark
Can mark thee not, my angel, nor shall I
Dare tread to harm what charmed Another's eye.

L'ho visto

O pious soul, the whole of human kind
Upon thy suff'ring drew, for Calvary
In thee stood o'er the world, and in thy mind
The sins here unconfessed glared merrily.
And 'yond the tombèd years thy vision still
In glory's bosom seers each plaintive breast
That on thee cries, for skies here bend at will
At thy fond asking, hard by godhead pressed.
O phantom not at rest, blest ghost not made
of spectred vagabondage seeking prayer,
But coming here withal, thou canst not fade
As quickly as thy years, but standing there
In perfumed gloriole, thou teachest me
How at this grille to see, how all to see.

(San Quirico, confessing for hours)

Pious soul: Blessed Padre Pio appeared last year to one fairly young lady, quite
unexpectedly. On the anniversary of the occurrence,
he gave another sign – a cross of light.

She died without the sacraments

*(Funeral Mass at Seggiano: none called
in time, that she might be shriven first.)*

There hovers heavy mystery above
A bier that here we set for e'er at rest.
Alas, alas, a molecule of love
In early days held days, all days, unblest.
None called in time, timed soul, and none was there
With stole and pow'r to steal from stolen years
The matter of a worry ling'ring e'er
Upon a coffin sealed with heavy fears.
O pow'r of sound of tickings untoward
That onward o'er long æons ever go
And backward may not walk! O! moments hard
In which were marred a million – but to know,
Hid soul, the whole in time, 'twould have timed all
In fregatura high all Hell t'appal.

Gloria hæc est omnibus sanctis eius

O volume that I wind and seal at last,
O rotula with many souls enrolled,
Each merry one eternity to blast
With glory high by one shy story told:
'Tis dense with commas and full periods marked
Upon the map of Chronos where no man
May trespass or undo an æon sparked
By pain and gain that demons all did fan.
Fly high, my brethren; call where gazing faints,
For though I know a fondness that hath fear
To let all go but God, the plod of Saints
From dust to stardust conquered draws me near,
And I shall yield this morsel, this last sigh,
If fondness unto madness may draw nigh.

(Completing years' work on Martyrology)

Two tombs

Two hollows side by side where morrows long
Commence their onward journey, ne'er to cease,
In parallel, in Hell or Heav'n; in song
Or howling o'er long harrowing; in peace
Or wanting but a moment evermore,
For that no priest did come – no priest like this
That calmly shut his eyes upon this store
Of moments weighed and gathered unto bliss...
O! mystery where history lies still
In characters indelible upon
The book of all that live – O! flick of Will
That will or will not go where all have gone
But only did they will, for till the end,
That end ne'er can, a man no hour may mend.

(At 3.00 a.m., concerned for the lady at Seggiano,
whom we buried next to a faithful priest friend.)

O Thing!

O Thing that has no name, O Mystery
Beyond the yonder land where all is well
Or not so well, where ancient History
Is long in its unwriting, Heav'n and Hell
Upon a moment pending, vending all
In calling Will that still could turn the tide
Of æons ere they came and e'er went on
Upon a tracèd course high bound and tied
Unto a distant second ever gone –
O Thing without a name, whose fame is bright
In regions where no sight may penetrate,
I spent some moons a-roving in thy light
Unveiled and hailed afar, for at this gate
Upon a manuscript I pored awhile
And heard a noisèd land where demons smile.

> *Manuscript*: The letter from Hell and the Purgatory
> Manuscript, translated in France.
> (Cf Ave Maria Press, Middletown, Co. Armagh.)

The author, at present living as a hermit in Duleek, Co. Meath, Ireland, has been living the monastic life for many years, and, since 1980, has been keeping a poetic journal, of which this volume, covering the years 1995-2000 (with a few poems from 2001), is an extract. His case caused some interest in the field of Carthusian spirituality, as it turned out to be a test-case for the fundamental question: Is literary activity compatible with the purely contemplative life? Under the Superiors of his Carthusian period (1976-1984), it was considered to be incompatible, and he was advised not to insist with regard to Solemn Vows. However, the question was examined subsequently both inside and outside the Order. This was pursued by Dom Augustin Devaulx, O. Cart., who made a massive study of Carthusian poets throughout the centuries, concluding with the work of Dom David, and adding a personal comment in his dedication, to the effect that there were many verses, but only one poet; by Dr James Hogg, who had lived for several years in the same Carthusian monastery, and by Dr Eva Schmid-Mörwald, who wrote an entire volume on the question. His verse has also aroused some discussion within literary circles, as his deliberate choice of elevated and at times archaic diction is not easily accepted. It has, however, been pointed out (in Wales, notably) that the problem does not arise either in his Welsh or in his French verse. This may be an indication of natural elevation of the Welsh language, and its influence upon the author's English may certainly be detected in this volume, as can that of the bardic heritage of which it is a natural part. In the words of Chateaubriand, "Le chant naturel de l'homme est triste". If there are moments in which ink and tears mingle, they owe their existence to the passage of high currents that settle with difficulty on the page. But the reader is warned: to be read, marked and inwardly digested, they need to be absorbed in the same spirit as that in which they found their way to the paper, and that implies silence and solitude. For poetry, as we know, is emotion recollected in tranquillity.